LAST VOYAGE AND BEYOND

Ian M. Malcolm

Published in 2017 by
Moira Brown
Broughty Ferry
Dundee. DD5 2HZ
www.publishkindlebooks4u.co.uk

Last Voyage and Beyond was first published
as a kindle book in 2013.

ISBN 978-1-5217-6537-1

I was a 1st Radio Officer/Purser with Alfred Holt & Co. of Liverpool, who owned the Blue Funnel Line and the Glen Line, and had requested a voyage to Australia before I swallowed the anchor. Calverley, who dealt with R/Os, had appointed me to the *Deucalion*, but said that Reg Peaston, who was to sail on the maiden voyage of the *Ixion*, was ill and that I could have her if had not recovered in time.

On Tuesday, 12 December, 1950, I caught the 2.15pm train from Liverpool Exchange Station, arrived in Glasgow at 8.30pm and went out to the ship at King George V Dock in Shieldhall. There is nothing more depressing than an almost deserted ship on a winter's night and, looking for a bit of company, I found the 3rd Mate in his cabin studying Latin. His name was J.T.H. Bennion and, although I was interrupting his studies, he made me welcome and explained that he was set on entering university. Mr Bennion left the ship two days later and I have an idea that he became a padre and went on to run a seamen's mission in the Far East.

The next morning, I went to the Mercantile Marine Office and signed the Articles which were Home Trade and '...not to extend beyond the expiration of the period of six months from the date of the agreement...'. I spent the evening with my friends, Marie and Stuart Crabb, at their home in Ibrox and travelled home to Dundee on the afternoon of Saturday, 16 December, to get my deep-sea gear.

I had no idea that a radio officer was employed by Dundee Harbour Trust, to communicate between the docks and the *Abertay Lightship*, until the tragic death of Mr James D Greenhill, aged 29, was reported in the Courier that day. He had been taking a bath in the Earl Grey Dock gatehouse at the end of the day's work and, as the bathroom was unheated, had installed a three-bar electric fire on a shelf above the bath. It was deduced that he had inadvertently pulled the flex, the heater had fallen into the bath and he was electrocuted. Although I felt it irreverent to go after the job so soon after the tragedy, I went to the docks on Monday afternoon and was interviewed by a middle-aged man who turned out to be the head shipwright. It was one of those interviews where the attitude of the interviewer tells you that you have no chance and that someone else is already lined up for the job. The man, who knew nothing about radio, asked me if I had experience of VHF (Very High Frequency). I truthfully answered that I had not, but, when I asked what difference that made, he made no comment. Mr Greenhill, who had been in the Merchant Navy prior to taking the job in

1942, was the only son of the well-known Dundee chemist whose shop was in the Overgate.

On rejoining the ship on Tuesday, 19 December, I was told that Captain Kerr was now on board and felt it polite to introduce myself. He was in his cabin and when I said, "Good afternoon, sir, I'm the purser", he gruffly replied, "Well, what about it?" I had never before met with such rudeness, said, "Good afternoon" and left.

Another display of rudeness was shown by a charge-hand when I was down a hold with the 4th Mate one day. As cases with Melbourne printed on them were being stowed so that the name was hidden, the young lad asked the dockers to rectify this. But, when they started to turn the cases round, a charge hand told them to pay no attention to the officer and they did. More careful stowage took up more of their time and the charge hand was not interested in facilitating discharge.

The *Deucalion* was not due to sail until Tuesday, so that I was able to go home for the weekend. My brother, Eric, met me at the station when the train got in about 7pm on the Saturday, the shops were still open and he went with me to buy a Parker 51 fountain pen. They were all the rage at the time and my parents were giving me one as a present. Then, after a brief visit home, we spent the evening at the Palais.

Helen, my girlfriend, was home from London on leave and, on having tea in her house the following evening, Christmas Eve, I met her Aunt Ester who had lived for many years in Budge Budge on the River Hooghli until her husband, John Norman, a river pilot, had been killed on board at ship at the wharf in 1944. Her son Ian, also present, was about to return to India as a clerk in a Calcutta jute mill. He was expected to be away for two or three years, but it turned out that he didn't like it, his mother paid his passage home and he was back in Dundee before I returned from my deep-sea voyage!

Christmas Day saw me on the 8am train to Glasgow and I travelled in the company of a workman, as Christmas was not then a holiday in Scotland. Marie and Stuart Crabb had invited me to lunch and it was late afternoon before I went down to the ship. Almost everyone was on board now and a group of us had a singsong with me playing the mouth organ. Glasgow was in the grip of one of those dense fogs which used to occur before the anti-pollution laws banned the use of coal fires in the city. We were to sail at 9.30am on Boxing Day, but, due to the fog, it was 12.30pm before we got away. The 2nd R/O was J.S. Sutherns.

We docked at No.2 Shed Gladstone Dock, Liverpool, at 9.30am the following day and I was told I could go home for the New Year! Holts were good when ships were in home ports during the Festive Season; they tried to let Scotsmen have the New Year at home and the others have Christmas. But, as the *Deucalion* had been in Glasgow for Christmas, I had the best of both worlds as I had done two years previously when on the *Eurybates*. Again I travelled on the overnight train from Lime Street and arrived in Dundee in the early afternoon of the next day. I went to bed, but was up to meet Helen downtown at 7 o'clock and we went to the Kings Cinema.

The New Year turned out to be the best I ever had. Helen and others had tea at my house, but shortly after tea, one of the lads' mothers came up to collect him because his grandmother had died. When they had gone, my mother remarked that she didn't see any sense in this as it was only spoiling his night when there was nothing he could do. And my grandfather, who was 82, joked about how inconsiderate some people were, dying at the New Year! Helen and I left for her house, about 11.30pm, and just before midnight, I, being dark-haired, was made to go out again and come in as their first-foot. And the rest of the night was spent first-footing.

My parents always spent New Year's Day with friends who were custodians of the Comerton (Children's) Home near Newport and Eric and I were shattered when Mother roused us at 10.30am. After a good meal and dancing to music provided by the pianola, he and I recrossed on the ferry to Dundee and went to the Palais with Helen. It was after 2am before I got to bed and even later/earlier the next day.

Departing on the 9.40pm train for Liverpool, I brought Helen to the house about 7pm. Grandad was there to say goodbye and when Mother and Dad, Eric and Helen and I were leaving, he broke down as he hugged me and said, "I'll maybe no' be here when you get back." I had gone away often enough before, but, on the station platform, I could see that was taking Mother all her time to hold back the tears. And when I received a letter from Helen before we sailed, she said that I had 'looked the cheeriest member of the party'! I think I was. I had had a great time at home and I was looking forward to seeing Australia.

As usual, I had to change trains at Perth and Preston, but although all trains were busy, I was lucky enough to have a seat all the way. The train arrived in Lime Street Station about an hour late, but I had breakfast and cleaned myself up at Atlantic House before reporting at the Office.

Calverley informed me that Reggie Peaston had recovered from his illness and that I was going on the *Deucalion*. She had been due to sail on Saturday, but sailing was now postponed until Monday. After Dr Wilson had passed me fit, Calverley asked me to renew my two-year contract with the Company under the Merchant Navy Established Service Scheme, but I refused on the grounds that I did not intend remaining at sea for that length of time. He tried to persuade me by saying it benefited the Company and that I would be released whenever I wished. But, considering that I could be held by the contract, I remained adamant and he wasn't pleased. I made a point of telling him how Captain Kerr had behaved when I reported to him in Glasgow and said, "If that's how he's going to behave, I don't think we're going to get on very well together." As usual, I just got the blank stare, but as Calverley had done pretty well by me, I gave him a copy of a photograph I had taken of Blue Funnel ships in line in Glasgow. Although he thanked me for it, this too brought no reaction. I could never get close to Calverley. I then went to sign on the *Deucalion* as 1st Radio Officer although, as usual, my main job was that of Purser and I didn't keep a wireless watch.

Although I had never before experienced it, it was apparently the policy to have all pursers go round the various departments in the Office, to acquaint them of any new developments. I met Ron Gallop and he and I went round together. Ron had been my No.1 during my first voyage on the *Glengarry* and we had got on well together. He was joining the *Astyanax* (GMSR), which was sailing for the Far East on Saturday, and we had lunch together at Atlantic House. I went back there for tea and visited a news cinema before going down to the ship in Gladstone Dock.

Friday was again spent in India Buildings going round the departments with Ron. The 3rd Engineer and I went into town on Saturday afternoon and I bought the three Pelican volumes of the 'Lives of the Great Composers', edited by AL Bacharach. On Sunday, the 2nd Sparks and I went to a news cinema.

I wrote five letters from Liverpool and sent £10 to the ROU (Radio

Officers' Union) to bring my subscriptions up to date. With my letter home, I enclosed my Allotment Note for £12 a month, explaining that this left me plenty to spend in Australia. I also mentioned that I had £16-10/- in notes although we werc legally permitted to take only £5 in notes and £2 in silver out of the country. I said that, until 14 January, letters should be addressed to the ship c/o Wm Stapledon & Sons, Port Said and from then until the 19th, c/o Luke, Thomas & Co., Aden. And after that, to write c/o Alfred Holt, Liverpool with stamps covering the appropriate rate to Australia affixed. I concluded my letter by saying that 'flu' was so prevalent in Merseyside that Birkenhead schools were not reopening until the 15th.

Monday, 8 January, 1951 was sailing day and I wrote a letter to Holts regarding the Ship's Library, supplied by the Seafarers' Education Service, of which I was the librarian. In the letter, I said, "When this ship docked in Liverpool on December 27th the library was intact, but when I rejoined the vessel on January 4th it was noticed that a new lock was on the library case and it was evident that the old lock had been forced. A workman tells me that the new lock was put on January 2nd, so that the missing books must have been taken between December 27th and January 2nd. The missing books are as follows: (and listed the sixteen books.)"

It was raining cats and dogs in the evening when Mr Nuttall arrived from the Office to see that everything was all right with me. He was an ex R/O and he told me a story about Captain Kerr when they had been on the Pacific run together before the war. Kerr, who was a big bruiser of a man, had been 2nd Mate at the time and very proud of his boxing ability. When they were in a western Canadian port, he had worn boxing gloves and, with another pair slung round his neck, had challenged anyone to take him on. It was lumbering country, a big Swede had accepted the challenge and 'knocked hell out of Kerr'. Nuttall laughed as he related the story so it seemed that Kerr had not been popular even then.

We sailed at 9.30pm and Darrell, the 2nd R/O, sent our [1] TR to Seaforthradio (GLV): 'GLV de GDQW (Our call sign) Deucalion QTO (leaving) Liverpool bnd Melbourne QSX (listening to) †Area 1A.' We broke down before we got out of the Mersey and it was hour or two before the engineers got us going again. A few hours later, when off Anglesey, the Mersey/Lynas Pilot went down a rope ladder into the Pilot Boat and it

---

[1] The name given to these reports. †Covered by Portishead Radio Station at Highbridge in Somerset and GLV would notified them, by teleprinter, that we were listening to their broadcasts.

was full away to Australia.

The *Deucalion* had been the *Glenogle*, built in Glasgow by Harland & Wolff in 1920, and was part of the Glen Line Fleet acquired by Holts in 1935. *Glenogle, Glenapp, Glengarry, Glenbeg*, and five other vessels of the same design, had been the largest oil burning ships in the world and all were twin-screw motor vessels. The *Glenogle*, which was renamed *Deucalion* in 1949, had a gross tonnage of 9513 and accommodation for twelve passengers. The previous *Deucalion* was the first vessel to be sunk in the Pedestal Convoy to Malta in August, 1942. She blew up shortly after being abandoned and some of her survivors later went on board the disabled *Ohio* to aid the exhausted crew. The other Glen Line ships listed above had been renamed as follows: *Glenapp* - *Dardanus* (GDXT) ; *Glengarry*, which had been renamed *Glenstrae* in 1939 to release her name for the ship building in Copenhagen - *Dolius* (GCXD); *Glenbeg* - *Dymas* (GBZK).

Captain W.K. Kerr was a 54-year-old bachelor from Ayr, known throughout the Company as 'Film Star' Kerr as he had played a leading role in the wartime film "Western Approaches". The film portrayed the danger confronting merchant seamen and the actors were serving Blue Funnel men. Kerr was the rudest master I ever sailed with, but largely due to the way I reacted to his rudeness, we got on tolerable well. When, years later, I played golf with a man who had worked for Mansfield & Co in Singapore, he told me that he and his wife had been passengers on a ship commanded by Kerr. Captain Stanger, whom I had coasted with on the *Medon*, and who was also of an irascible nature, had also been on the ship and he and Kerr never spoke to each other. Kerr had an Extra Master's Certificate.

The 1st Mate, who had a Master's Certificate, was 36-year-old E.G. Painter, from Sunderland and we got on well for most of the voyage.

Thomas Geoffrey Nelson, aged 25 was 2nd Mate. He came from Birkenhead and was a quiet pleasant man who also had a Master's Certificate.

The 3rd Mate, who had a 2nd Mate's Certificate, was 23-year-old Peter Overend from Bradfield in Essex. Peter was a tall cheerful chap who had acquired a girlfriend in Australia the previous voyage. He had a portrait of her on his desk and continually talked about her during the outward passage.

Three midshipmen were named in the Articles, which they did not sign, but the senior one, Ronald Morris from Liverpool who became 20 on 19 January, was promoted Acting 4th Mate the day we sailed. This left us with two middies; 18-year-old Nicholas Robinson from Colchester and 17-year-old William Roberts from Anglesey.

Darrell O'Byrne, my 19-year-old No.2, was a pleasant lad from Southport with a 2nd Class PMG Certificate. (I was 25 and had my 1st Class.)

H.D. (Denis) Hall, from Liverpool, was 30 and our Male Nurse. Denis was always cheerful and we became friends. Towards the beginning of the voyage, he told a story about something which happened to him when he was a ticket collector on the Liverpool Overhead Railway and, shortly after this, the 2nd Mate remarked to me, "You never know whom you're sailing with these days."!

T.A. Price, aged 47, was Chief Engineer and a pleasant enough man from Blackpool. He had a 1st Class Certificate (Steam and Motor).

C. Ligertwood, aged 30, was 2nd Engineer and a somewhat uncouth Glaswegian who lived in Cheshire. He had a 1st Class Certificate (Motor).

G.J. Walker, aged 24, the 3rd Engineer, from Clydebank, had a 2nd Class Certificate (Motor).

The 4th Engineer and three Assistant Engineers were all uncertificated: W.B. Leitch, aged 22 from Glasgow; R.L. Winthorpe, aged 21 from Birkenhead; K. Hirst, aged 21 from Huddersfield; Harry McD. Watson, aged 22 from Banff, but living in Humberstone near Leicester; H. Gardiner, aged 21 from Clydach near Swansea. Harry Watson, who was married and had a baby son, became my buddy on the ship.

The 1st Electrician was G.A. Thompson, aged 26, from Dundonald near Belfast, and the 2nd Electrician S. Wilson, aged 25, from Mordon, Co. Durham.

56-year-old J.T. Kirk from Liverpool was Chief Steward and 23-year-old J.H. Birch, also from Liverpool, was 2nd Steward.

The ratings, including the Carpenter, No.1 Fireman and Ship's Cook, were Chinese so that the total crew consisted of 22 Europeans and 55 Chinese. With our twelve passengers, there were 89 people on board.

Our monthly salaries, apart from the Master's, never shown on the Articles, were as follows:

1st Mate   £52
2nd Mate   £45
3rd Mate   £37
1st Radio Officer   £40 plus [2]£6 purser's bonus
2nd Radio Officer   £28-10/-
Male Nurse   £25
Chief Steward £42-10/-

---

[2] For the first two years as purser, the bonus was £4; after that it remained at £6 and was paid only while on Foreign Articles.

2nd Steward   £29
Chief Engineer £60
2nd Engineer   £54
3rd Engineer   £43
4th Engineer   £33
Asst Engineer £30
1st Electrician £40
2nd Electrician £36

Midshipmen's salaries, not shown on Articles, were £6-5/, £7-10/- and £13-5/- for 1st, 2nd and 3rd years of apprenticeship. There was a minimum and maximum rate for each job with increments paid for each year of service at a particular grade. Mates and Engineers were also paid according to certificates held, but this did not apply to radio officers.

The Chinese Carpenter, Bosun and Ship's Cook were each paid £20-18-6d. The sailors, firemen and stewards got £12-3-6d.

The weather was bad when we dropped the pilot and continued bad almost all the way to Port Said. It was rough indeed in the Biscay of Biscay and Mr Leigh, a passenger, was to be seen stoically assisting his wife to walk the deck in an attempt to overcome her seasickness.

We all had our own radio sets and listened to the BBC Home and Light Programmes until they faded as we headed south. After that, we tuned in to the BBC General Overseas Service on short-wave although music could be had, on medium wave, from first the French and then Spanish and Portuguese stations. It a somewhat similar story in the wireless room where Darrell kept watch on 500 kcs (600 metres); Landsendradio (GLD) and other British coast stations gradually gave way to the French, Spanish and Portuguese.

Only the shadowy outline of Cape Finisterre was seen until we rounded Cape St Vincent and the only land seen after passing through the Strait of Gibraltar on Saturday 13 January, was Cape Bon, in Tunisia, which was still littered with the wrecks left behind, in 1943, by the defeated Afrika Corps.

Under the direction of Captain Kerr, I kept the ship's Official Log. It was the custom to present it to the master every Monday morning and when I climbed the outside stairs to his cabin on our first Monday at sea, I found him sitting at his desk with his back to me. I knocked on the open door to attract his attention, but when he continued to ignore me, I said "I'll come back when you're not so busy, sir." This annoyed Kerr and he never did that to me again. I was told that he had had a Parker 51 fountain pen and, when it refused to function, had thrown it out of a porthole into the sea. I may say that my Parker 51, which I still have, proved equally poor. Monday morning was also the time when Kerr inspected the crew's accommodation and although I had previously seen only the Chief Steward accompany a master, Kerr had me join the inspection party on its rounds.

We dropped anchor in Port Said harbour at 7.06am on Saturday 20 January. The routine, which I have previously described elsewhere, got under way. A gentleman passenger left the ship and another took his place. Eric had admired the leather grip, which I had bought from a bumboatman in Port Said, and asked me get one for him. I got a suede one for 30 bob (£1.50). With a pilot on board, we weighed anchor at 11.30am and entered the Canal in a convoy of several ships. The passage through the Canal was slow and it was 5.42am the next day before exited and anchored in Suez Bay.

We had a cat on board and Captain Kerr wanted rid of it because a £25 deposit had to be paid on all cats on ships arriving in Australian ports. If the cat were found to be missing when the ship left, the deposit was lost. The Agent had come out in his launch from Port Tewfik and, when he was returning to the shore, Kerr had a middy take the cat and go with him to see that the animal was landed. This was done, but when the launch came out to the ship a few hours later, the cat leapt from it, shot up the gangway and could not be found before the launch departed again! But, in Melbourne, Kerr got over the problem by signing a form stating that we had no cats on board. Cats used to travel the world on ships before regulations were introduced to prevent them doing so. Because of engine repairs, we didn't sail until 3.36pm.

A copy of the English language 'Egyptian Mail', dated Sunday, 21, 1951, given to me by the Agent, contained the following items of news:

The Korean War was in progress and the main heading was "U.N. ARMY HAS 'PLENTY OF FIGHT IN IT'". - General Eisenhower, now the Supreme Commander of the Atlantic Pact Army, was back in Germany and saying 'Let bygones be bygones'. - John Strachey, War Minister in the Labour Government, was defending rearming Britain. - Dr Edith Summerskill, Minister of National Insurance, was concluding her week's tour of Egypt's social centres. - British hospitals were under a great strain due to Europe's influenza epidemic and the disease appeared to have entered Britain via a Swedish ship which called at Liverpool towards the end of 1950. - India was so short of food-grains that the ration had been cut and wheat was being imported from Canada. - On 26 January, the BBC were to celebrate 'Australia Day' with a special 'Hallo, Australia" programme in which Kitty Bluett and Bill Kerr were to appear. (Kitty Bluett was a regular performer in "Ray's a Laugh" and Bill Kerr later took part in the "Hancock's Half-Hour" series.) - Dr Kenneth Oakley of the British Museum for Natural History, had told BBC listeners of 'a newly devised test which helps to date fossil bones'. The test had been applied to the Piltdown Skull and scientists were in dispute as to whether it was half a million or fifty thousand years old. (It turned out to be a fake.)

As it was winter in the Northern Hemisphere, we didn't change into tropical uniform until Tuesday, 23 January when we were in the Red Sea. The *Glenroy* (GPPN), on her way to the Far East, passed us, out of sight, the same day and I had a 'chinwag" on the 'air' with Geoff White who had been my No.1 on the *Glengarry* when I had made my second voyage on her as No.2. Mocking our slowness, Geoff said that they would be back home in three months to which I replied, "Here playing deck tennis" which was something never done on the fast Glen boats.

The weather was now lovely and we played deck tennis every day from 4pm until dinner at 6pm. We mixed with the passengers, which we seldom did on the *Glengarry*, and Mrs Leigh became my partner in tournaments. I really enjoyed the games although, because of the unaccustomed exercise, my legs and hips ached after the first bout. The court was marked out on the starboard side of the main deck, beside No.4 hatch, and the idea of the game is to throw a quoit/circular piece of rope over the net so that your opponents fail to catch it. If it lands in their court, you score a point. The top of the net was at a height of about five feet and another net was strung along the ship's side to prevent the quoit from being thrown into the sea.

The wireless room receiver broke down on Wednesday, 24 January and I spent that day and the next studying the circuit diagram and testing components. We had only the one receiver, the circuit data was incomplete, there were no spares other than some valves and no proper tools to effect repairs. The Chief Engineer and the Electricians kindly asked if they could be of any assistance, but I managed to clear the fault by about 10pm on Thursday. I thought it prudent, however, to have a radio engineer examine the set in Aden, as I didn't relish another breakdown on the long haul from Aden to Melbourne.

We anchored off Aden's Steamer Point at 4.30am on Friday and I received a letter from Eric telling me that my pal, John Noble, had become engaged. A young radio engineer came out to the ship in the forenoon. He couldn't locate any fault and said, "I'm afraid there's no more I can do. It's working all right at the moment and you'll just have to hope it keeps that way." But as I was the one who had the 6445 mile passage to Melbourne ahead of me with a receiver which could breakdown at any time, I replied, "There's only one thing in the power pack which we haven't been able to check. That's the rectifier (valve) and we haven't got a spare one so that we can check it. How about going ashore and collecting one from your stores?" He did and the receiver gave no further trouble. But, as he was unable to supply a spare, I resolved to get another rectifier in Melbourne.

With our fuel oil bunkers and fresh water supply replenished, we sailed at 1.06pm.

Our passengers were a much friendlier breed than those carried to and from Malay and Hong Kong. The Hong Kong passengers not so bad, but the Singapore lot were generally snobbish and seldom communicated with the crew unless bad weather was encountered. On top of this, the design of the fast Glen ships militated against them mixing with the officers, whereas that of the *Deucalion* facilitated it. Our passengers were:

Mr and Mrs Cowan, an elderly couple from County Londonderry. I believe Mr Cowan was a farmer. Mrs Cowan was Australian and they were going to Australia on holiday.

Mr and Mrs Leigh from Chester. Mr Leigh was an accountant and keen on emigrating to Australia. Mrs Leigh, a teacher, was less sure about this and they were going, together with their 15-year-old daughter, Dorothy, to spend some time in Australia before making a decision. They were particularly friendly with George, the 1st Electrician, and Dorothy was having the time of her life with the attention she received from all the boys.

Miss Jones was a 32-year-old stenographer returning home to Sydney after a spell in Europe. Some of the boys maintained that Miss Jones, a smoker with red fingernails, wore falsies!

Mr and Mrs Sainsbury were a young honeymoon couple from the London area. Mr Sainsbury had been appointed a lecturer in sociology at the University of Adelaide. He and I had the occasional conversation, but I never got more than a 'good morning' out of his wife.

Mr and Mrs Paine were another elderly couple going on holiday and Mrs Paine was Australian.

Mr Rix, who had joined at Port Said, was a shipping clerk going home. At first sight, I thought he was the type who would mix with the crew, but he didn't. Whether the weather was hot or cold, he always wore the same sports jacket and one morning Denis said, "Tell that bloke to report to the dispensary at 9 o'clock to have that jacket removed."!

A large man with white hair, whose name I can't recall, made up our complement of twelve passengers. He had been in the trenches of France during the First World War and suffered badly from trench foot; a form of frostbite which smote many of the troops by standing for long periods in cold water. Because of this, he had specially constructed shoes but, throughout the passage, wore carpet slippers.

Holts divided their ships into two classes according to their speed, amenities and the standard of accommodation provided. The single fares from the UK to Australia were:

	'A' Fares		'B' Fares
	From	To	
Fremantle	£108	£144	£91
Adelaide	£114	£150	£93
Melbourne	£117	£153	£94
Sydney	£120	£156	£95
Brisbane	£123	£159	£96

The food was excellent on all the ships and all passengers were deemed to be 1st Class. The *Deucalion* was in the category 'B' and the *Ixion* in category 'A'. On the 28000-ton Orient Liner *Orcades*, which took 28 days from London to Melbourne, the Tourist "B" fare was in the region of £60.

The crossing of the Indian Ocean was generally rough, but, when the weather allowed it, we played deck tennis and also deck quoits - a game preferred by the less agile. Captain Kerr had become more mannerly towards me and one day when I was involved in a game of deck tennis, he called out from his small deck above where we played, "Mr Malcolm, I'd like to see you when you've finished your game, but finish your game first." On another occasion when I was watching a game in progress and holding a glass of cider, he called out, "Mr. Malcolm, who are you saving that drink for?" Without thinking, I had not drunk from the glass and deduced that he thought I was holding it for one of the midshipmen who were not allowed alcoholic beverages!

One dark evening I was standing beside Darrell in the wireless room when Midshipman Robinson burst in out of breath. The wireless room was on the boat deck and Kerr, standing on his deck at the rear of the forward accommodation, had thought he had seen Miss Jones enter it and sent Nick to put a stop to any hanky-panky! On another night, when I really was with Miss Jones, she pointed out the stars in Orion's belt and referred to them as the saucepan; a term I had never before heard. The easily identified Southern Cross had been seen since the Red Sea.

As Captain Kerr behaved towards the passengers as he did towards the crew, they did not like him. In the saloon, they all sat at one long table. Kerr was at the head of the table, beside Mr Price, the Chief Engineer, and Mr Painter, the 1st Mate, sat at the foot, near the table at which I sat with the other mates. Kerr always entered the saloon by the wide staircase which descended directly into it and hung his cap on the bottom post before crossing to take his seat. When the passengers said, "Good morning, Captain", they got only a grunt in return. But Kerr was something of an enigma. He painted the most excellent miniature marine watercolours and I believe he gave one to a passenger. He was also a keen golfer, had his clubs with him and was often seen on his small deck hitting a ball attached to a long piece of string.

The Indian Ocean is a big ocean and throughout our diagonal crossing from Aden, we heard and communicated with only the Australia bound *Chanda* and a Panamanian, proceeding in the opposite direction, whose British Sparks informed us that he was earning about twice as much as I was. I had never known the ether to be so quiet since the days of the wartime convoys and it gave the impression that we were alone in that vast expanse of water.

The *Deucalion* was equipped with only a medium wave transmitter, with a daylight range of only 200 to 300 miles, and one day in the saloon, Mr Painter leaned across to me and said, "Mr Malcolm, the passengers are asking if we are in touch with Australia yet?" My reply that we were in touch with nobody must have shattered their confidence.

Until we left the Red Sea, our Area Transmitting and Receiving Station was Portisheadradio (GKL, etc.). In the Indian Ocean it was Colombo (GZH), Ceylon until we reached 95°15′ East when it became Sydney (VIS), Australia. We listened to the traffic lists sent by our Area Station at set times and, if our call sign were in a list, continued to listen until the message was transmitted. But not having an H/F (high frequency/short wave) transmitter, we could acknowledge receipt only through another ship within range which had H/F. Likewise, we had to send messages to these stations via an H/F ship and, if we had been required to do so during that passage, it would have been almost impossible. After the closure of the Area System in 1972 all ships required an H/F transmitter in order to communicate directly with the station of destination.

For some unknown reason, the purser was not involved in the checking out of cargo consigned to Australian ports other than Fremantle and Adelaide and, as we were not going to either, I had no check books to write up from manifests. This left me with time to return to the BIET (British Institute of Engineering Technology) City and Guilds correspondence course which I had had to abandon when on the Far East run. Studying was done, however, in a half-hearted and spasmodic fashion as, due to my lack of proficiency in higher mathematics, I now regretted having bought the course and I had come to the conclusion that my bent was more in the literary field.

I had read Jack London's 'Mutiny of the Elsinore' before Aden and, between there and Australia, the lives of Bach, Beethoven, Handel, Liszt and Chopin in the 'Lives of the Great Composers' I had bought in Liverpool. Eric had given me a book listing all the recent classical recordings and, when I heard a work being performed on the radio, I made a note against it as to whether or not it appealed to me.

In case of emergency, a chit, giving our noon position, was sent to the wireless room daily by the 2nd Mate, and the following, recorded in my diary, shows our progress across the Indian Ocean.

Wednesday, 31 January, 2°16′N 65°15′E; Saturday, 3 February, 6°08′S 76°56′E; Sunday, 4 February, 9°19′S 80°43′E; Monday, 5 February, 12°16′S 84°43′E - just west of the Cocos Islands; Tuesday 6 February, the day of the New Moon and Chinese New Year celebrated by our crew, 15°03′S 87°43′E; Wednesday, 7 February, 17°49′S 91°30′E - that night I was able to listen to the local radio station in Geraldton in Western Australia, whose position is 28°44′S 114°37′E, and also to Perth; Thursday, 8 February, 20°08′S 94°35′E; Friday, 9 February, 22°23′S 97°35′E. By Sunday, 11 February, it was cool enough for us to change back into blues/blue uniform.

Darrell copied a weather report being transmitted by a ship to a land station in numbered code. There was a codebook in the chart room, but when Mr Painter and I tried to decode the message and arrived at the word 'snow', we gave it up as a bad job! It became more and more difficult to continue with the deck tennis. Mrs Leigh and I got through to the second round of a tournament, but were knocked out by the pair who eventually won. By 17 February, I was still in the quoits tournament with another partner, but, due to the bad weather, I don't think it was completed or that anyone got the 10/- (50p) prize money.

As we neared the west coast of Australia, there was a day of such torrential rain that speed was reduced. And I never saw another ship leak as the *Deucalion* did. When we went in for dinner that night, there were buckets and basins all over the saloon floor and the stewards were attempting to sweep away the water which was sloshing about all over the place. The passengers were nearly washed out of their cabins on the upper deck, but our cabins remained dry. Ironically, our fresh water supply was becoming so low that we were asked to conserve it and I believe Captain Kerr even considered putting in at Fremantle for some.

It was much cooler than I had expected when we rounded Cape Leeuwin and crossed the Great Australian Bight so that I slept under two blankets. It was a very different story ashore, however, as I heard a local radio station announcer say, that, for the fifth time that summer, the thermometers in Melbourne were reading over 100°F. Unlike Britain at the time, Australia had many commercial radio stations with anything from cornflakes to pianos advertised at intervals. But, as in Britain now, there was the option of listening to the stations of the ABC (Australian Broadcasting Commission); the equivalent of the BBC.

When I passed the sheet round to ascertain what each man wanted to draw in Melbourne, almost all the Chinese, but particularly the deckhands and stewards, put down for more than they had in their accounts. They had all left allotments and had received a month's advance of wages when they joined. And, after taking their Steward's Accounts, for tobacco, drinks, etc. into consideration, they were left in the red. All accepted my explanation except Ma Poo, the Carpenter who allotted £10 a month, half his salary, to his wife in Singapore. He became very distraught, babbled on incomprehensibly in his pidgin English and I just could not get through to him. It was all too easy for a purser to allow men to overdraw, but I would never allow this as it always led to trouble in the end. I decided to give each man £2 which did not make a great deal of difference to their accounts and kept them happy. Some time later, and against my protestations, Ma Poo insisted on making a wooden box to hold my radio and I still use it to hold letters which I received and wrote while at sea.

I began writing a letter on the night of Saturday, 17 February when the ship was rolling in a heavy swell, coming right in on our beam, and the spray coming high over the decks. Our ETA at Port Phillip Heads was noon the next day, but there was considerable doubt about this due to the weather and we had heard on the radio that the *Strathaird* and other vessels were anchored off the Heads unable to enter. On Monday night, when we were about sixty miles from the Heads and land loomed out of the murk, Captain Kerr turned south to seek the safety of the open sea. This eased the rolling, but we were back in roughly the same place on Tuesday morning and didn't reach the Heads until 6pm. Later that evening I heard Melbourne radio announce, "The 10000-ton Blue Funnel liner *Deucalion* is lying outside the Heads tonight, but is unable to enter because the pilot boat cannot put a man on board due to rough seas." It certainly was rough and Kerr said it was the worst passage he had experienced.

On Tuesday, 20 February, the (Melbourne) Sun reported:

'More than 30 passengers on the coastal ship Kanimbla received broken bones or severe cuts while she lay outside the Heads during Sunday's storm. Scores more received minor injuries. Many people were injured on the Taroona, which also was held outside the Heads. The ships were due on Sunday, but berthed yesterday. Passengers said that while the ships were waiting for the weather to allow them to enter the Bay - Sixty-foot rollers crashed over the ships. The Taroona, although only a few hundred yards away often disappeared from sight of the Kanimbla. Almost the entire ships' complements were seasick. Furniture smashed in the lounges and hundreds of pieces of glassware and crockery were destroyed. ....

The Strathaird, which also was due on Sunday, was held out in the Bay all day yesterday because of winds too strong for berthing. Hundreds of people waited on Station Pier for her from 7a.m. until after dark." The 'paper also reported that the former Bass Strait passenger ship Nairana (3400 tons), which had been anchored in the Bay for three years awaiting a buyer, had been blown aground. She was now 2ft higher in the water than her floating depth and firmly wedged in the sand.'

The sea had moderated when a pilot boarded at 8.30am on Wednesday, 21 February and took us through the Heads, between Points Lonsdale and Nepean, into Port Phillip Bay. It was a relief to sail in calm waters and under a blue sky before we anchored at 12.48pm. An immigration officer came out to the ship and, from the crew list, checked all the Chinese individually. Although Australia was crying out for immigrants, it operated what was called a 'White Australia' policy and they were taking no chances that a non-white might 'jump ship'. The *Ixion* was anchored close to us. She had passed through the Heads directly ahead of us although she had left the Mersey twelve days after we had. We were taken alongside at Williamstown at 4pm and I stood beside Mrs Leigh at the rail when we were being tied up to the quay. When I said to her that it didn't seem all that long since we left Liverpool, she chased me. A poor sailor, she had suffered from seasickness whenever the weather had been bad throughout the forty-three day passage; the longest I ever experienced.

That same day, the *Diomed* (GCYR) sailed for Glasgow.

A Government Wireless Inspector boarded and, after he had examined the equipment, we were yarning about music in my cabin when Mr Sainsbury, the University Lecturer, came in and took issue with me on some point. The Inspector gestured towards the 'Lives of the Great Composers' on my bookshelf as he said, "He should know something about it."

All our passengers disembarked at Williamstown which is more or less a suburb of Melbourne. Those who were going on to Sydney, had the choice of going by either air or rail. The distance by air is 440 miles and the fare was £6-6/-. By rail, the distance is 590 miles. The 1st Class fare was £9-5-3d and the 2nd Class fare £5-8-3d. The rate of exchange was £1 Australian to 16/- (80p) sterling. I may add that the 'flu epidemic had been so bad in Europe that anyone landing in Australia suffering from it was immediately put into quarantine.

When our Agent, representing John Sanderson & Co., brought mail on board shortly after we docked in Williamstown, I received a letter from my mother which contained a shock. My grandfather, who had been suffering from no more than what the doctor considered to be a bad cold, had died in his sleep during the early hours of Wednesday, 24 January. I remembered what he had said about folk being inconsiderate to die at the New Year and his prophetic words when he had said goodbye to me just three weeks before he died. He had lived in his house, on the landing below us, for fifty-two years and had been buried the day we called at Aden. I also received a lovely portrait of Helen which henceforth adorned my cabin. Peter Overend was another who received a shock that day; the girl, who had occupied his thoughts throughout the passage, had transferred her affections to another bloke.

The only cargo which we had for Williamstown was two railway locomotives, carried on the forward deck, and their tenders, carried on the after deck. These were discharged the following day and Harry Watson and I took the opportunity to go into Melbourne in the afternoon. When I asked a young man in Williamstown where the railway station was, he replied, "New Australian", signifying that he was a recent immigrant from Europe who didn't understand [3]English. Immigrants were pouring into Australia from all over Europe, but there was strong opposition to German immigrants from Jews and from trade union, church and university leaders who claimed that this was not a sectarian or religious issue, but that Australia's security was at stake. Australia was also scared of communism and the Communist Party Dissolution Act 1950 had made the Party illegal. Some months previously, all the major trade unions had begun proceedings to have the Act ruled invalid and, on Thursday, 8 March, they won their case.

In the evening, I went to a dance at the Seamen's Mission and, at its close, the band played a national anthem which I recognized, but could not name. When I asked the padre, he said it was the Dutch anthem and that it had been played in honour of the many Dutch seamen present. The tune was familiar to me because of my visits to the Netherlands the previous year.

---

[3] Today, almost 30% of Melbourne's population speaks a language other than English at home.

We were moved out to anchor again the next day as the port of Melbourne was so congested that we had to wait our turn to berth. This irked us as the fifth and final Test Match in the England v Australia series was being played in Melbourne and we were afraid we might miss the chance of seeing it. We listened to the radio commentary every day while at anchor and eventually berthed at Victoria Dock at 9.30am on Wednesday, 28 February. The teams were:

Australia	England
Hassett(Captain)	Brown(Captain)
Tallon(Wicketkeeper)	Evans(Wicketkeeper)
Morris	Bailey
Burke	Bedser
Harvey	Tattersall
Miller	Compton
Johnston	Hutton
Lindwall	Simpson
Johnson	Sheppard
Iverson	Washbrook
Hole	Wright

1st Innings score: 217   320

Cash had to be paid out to the crew, but I thought I could leave Darrell to do this for once so we tossed to see which of us would go to our first day of the Test Match; whoever lost would go next day. I won and this was fortunate for me as it turned out to be the final day of the Test. Harry, Denis and I were off the ship by 11.45am and at the cricket ground by 12.30pm. The second innings was in progress, with Australia batting first, and we saw Hole, Lindwall, Tallon, Johnston and Iverson dismissed. And, with Tallon left 'not out', this ended their innings.

England had already lost the Ashes by losing the four previous games, but they required only 95 runs to win the fifth and final Test and Hutton and Washbrook opened for England. Washbrook, caught by Lindwall, was dismissed for 7 runs. He was replaced by Simpson, run out for 15. Simpson was replaced by Compton and, with Hutton his partner at the wicket, the target was reached and England had won by 1 run and 8 wickets. On Thursday, 1 March, the Sun newspaper reported: "England's victory by eight wickets in the fifth Test yesterday was acclaimed by spectators in one of the happiest demonstrations seen on the Melbourne Cricket Ground. It was England's first Test victory against Australia since

1938. ....Brigadier Green, English joint manager, said: We are very happy and I would like to pay a tribute to the behaviour of Australian crowds. Everywhere they have been magnificent and shown wonderful impartiality. ...." And, concerning the behaviour of the crowd of 21731 on that final day, I would heartily concur with this view.

At one point in the game, I stood beside a man who, in shirtsleeves, braces and soft hat, looked typical Australian and asked me where I came from. When I said, "Dundee", he said he too came from there and went on to reminisce about such places as the Wellgate Steps. Unlike British spectators, the Australians heckled the players in good fun. When Hutton attempted to hit a wide ball and missed, a man called out, "Who do you think you are? Hutton?"

The game ended just after 5pm. Harry had to go back to the ship, but Denis and I had tea in a restaurant and then, looking for entertainment, stumbled across the stage performance of 'Oklahoma' at His Majesty's Theatre. No doubt our long spell at sea heightened our enjoyment of the show, but we thought it absolutely wonderful.

There was a large double page leaflet advertising the band of the Black Watch inside the programme, but when I returned to my seat after the interval, it wasn't there. I was hunting high and low for it when the girl sitting behind me eventually handed it to me saying, "Is this what you're looking for?" and then admitted that she had been looking at my programme while we were away. The Black Watch band, under the direction of Bandmaster L.H. Hicks, were on their first visit to Australia and New Zealand and performing at the Town Hall.

On Saturday, 3 March, the Newmarket Handicap was being run at Flemington Racecourse. Harry and I went with Peter Overend who then drifted off on his own. We had lost on the big race and on every other before it was time for the Newmarket Stakes. Only three horses were entered; Alistair, the favourite, Midway and Zethos. Harry handed me his half-crown saying, "Put it on what you like and don't tell me." It was almost a photo finish between Alistair and Midway and when Harry saw Zethos coming in well behind, he said, "I bet that's our horse". And it was! We met Peter when we were all strap-hanging on the crowded train back into town, but, although looking miserable due to having lost £10, he said he intended returning for the Australian Cup the following Saturday. Australians are mad keen on racing. When a wharfie (docker) saw the radio in my cabin, he asked if he could hear a racing commentary. I obliged, but when he returned the next day and I realized it was to be a daily occurrence, I was having no more of it.

Harry wanted to buy a mouth-organ for a friend and we entered a huge musical shop. A male assistant came to serve us and Harry asked for an Echo Vamper. When the assistant said they didn't have any, Harry pointed out that there was one in the glass case beside us. "Oh, Echo," said the man. "That's what I said," said Harry. Afterwards, Harry said to me, "*You* knew what I said." "Yes," I replied, "but I speak the same way that you do."

In the record department of the same store, we stood at a counter for ten minutes while the girl assistants yarned to customers and one little blond made a date on the phone. Finishing her conversation, the latter eventually came up to us and said, "Yes?" Harry said, "No" and the blond walked away in a huff. Out of the shop, I said to Harry, "You're a genius, Watson. I wait all that time to hear her saying YES and you saying NO."

Dance halls were the place to meet the girls in those days. When I went with a group to the Trocadero one evening, a girl refused to dance with one of us. For a laugh, others in the party then asked her, but she refused each one in turn! On another occasion, I spent the evening in the company of a girl who was studying psychology, journalism and art at the University. When she expressed an interest in the East, I impressed her by quoting from the Koran and, when her sister heard this, she asked if I were an Indian! Telling me that her sister was also at the University, the psychology student added, "She's clever too" and, although no doubt true, the implication amused me. Another amusing incident occurred when I was returning to the ship late one evening. I boarded what was the last tram at its terminus to find the conductress having difficulty with the only other passenger, who was drunk. Just before it was about to set off, the drunk got off again to get cigarettes from a kiosk about fifty yards away. The conductress seized the opportunity, gave two dings on the bell and the drunk was left waving frantically behind.

I met Mary Bowring, whose mother came from Edinburgh, at the Trocadero and on the afternoon of Sunday 4 March, went with her on a Parlorcars coach tour to the Dandenong Ranges. The outward journey was by way of Ringwood, Croydon and at Montrose the coach left the main road and climbed to Mount Dandenong which is 2077 feet high. From the observation platform, we had a panoramic view of the surrounding bush country with the scent of gum trees pervading the air. The hills, which are foothills of the Great Dividing Range, are called the Blue Dandenongs and, in the heat of the afternoon, they did look blueish. We returned through Olinda, Belinda and Upper Ferntree Gully and the trip, which left the City at 2pm and returned at 6pm, cost A12/-.

We left the coach at the park which houses the war memorial and walked through it into the beautiful botanic gardens. The gardens, which were immaculately kept, require no hothouses and we sat by a pond overhung by eucalyptus and other gum trees until the place closed at 8pm.

My paternal grandmother's maiden name was Ireland and, as my father had the idea that one of her family had started up a ships' chandler business in Melbourne, I looked up the telephone directory to see if there were one of that name. There was a florist with several branches in the City, but no ships' chandler. I later tried again in Sydney without success.

A rather surprising thing happened when I was on a tram into town one day. A young man sitting opposite me leaned across and asked, "Is your name Malcolm?" When I replied that it was, he said it was also his name. He was a sailor off the *Ixion* and said that he had recognized me as we had been on the Lifeboatman's Course in Liverpool together the previous year.

8   BY AIR TO SYDNEY, NSW, VIA CANBERRA, A.C.T.

The idea of visiting Sydney had formed in my mind while crossing the Indian Ocean. I asked Kerr's permission go for the weekend, he agreed and asked how much I expected it to cost. When I said about £20, he thought this an exorbitant amount and said, "And you're willing to spend £20 just to see Sydney?" I replied that I was and that this would be a lot cheaper than coming out again from the UK to see it!

Due to the time factor, flying was the only option. I rose at 5.30am on Saturday, 10 March. The hired car I had ordered collected me at 6 o'clock and took me to the office of Trans-Australia Airlines (TAA) in Swanston Street; in time to board the 6.35am Airline coach which connected with the 7.15am flight from Essendon Airport, about eight miles away. I later described the whole weekend in the letter I wrote home on 15 March and the following is a direct quote.

"At Essendon, we sat around in the waiting room for some little time and eventually boarded our aircraft - a (Douglas) Dakota DC3 - which mechanics, etc. had been making ready. After taxiing on the runway, with a great run we were off and in a couple of minutes had climbed to 7000 ft. Although this was my first experience of air travel, it did not, however, seem entirely new to me. We have often sat in cinemas looking out of the windows of an aircraft in flight and this I am sure serves to familiarize one with air travel. The experience was no more and no less than I had expected, although at the same time the feel of terra firma is, to me, more conducive to a sense of security! We flew over the open country surrounding Melbourne (not entirely, of course) across a section of the Gt. Dividing Range and touched down at Canberra, Capital of Australia, at 9.20am. A light breakfast had been served by the hostess and I had procured a souvenir flight log and some pictures - one of the latter showing the smoke rising from a bush fire. Canberra is a city in the making. From the air it can be seen to be spaced out in most orderly fashion over a large area and with the gleaming white Parliament House very much in evidence.

A coach again made the journey from airport to city, this time a distance of five miles. At the TAA office in Canberra I made enquiries about carrying on to Sydney in the afternoon. When booking at Melbourne I had been unable to book a seat from Canberra to Sydney, but had bought an 'open' ticket. The clerk had said I was taking a chance doing this, but he reckoned I would manage a seat on the 'plane. However, at Canberra, I learned that I could not get on any TAA 'plane to Sydney until Sunday night. This, of course, was useless, but the clerk at Canberra said to try at the office of Australian National Airways (ANA) further down the street. There they couldn't give me anything definite, but the clerk said the 3.30pm 'plane from Canberra to Sydney might leave Melbourne with a vacant seat. He wouldn't be able to tell me, however, until about 2 o'clock and the 'plane was in flight. This information received, I went off to see Canberra and by stopping at a shop for postcards, missed a tour of the place.

From the Civic Centre with its neatly kept lawn and gardens, I got a bus to the National War Memorial - a large building with a big dome which is a museum showing the history of Australian forces during World War I. I wandered through its halls, but not wasting a great deal of time on the exhibits.

When I left the War Memorial, it was to go to Parliament House which could be seen a little over a mile away and down a wide straight and dusty road. To get there by walking would have taken up too much time, so I got on a bus going in the wrong direction, got off at the next stop and boarded a bus in the right direction which took me on a circuitous route of about four miles before setting me down at Parliament House. The House itself was closed when I was there and the surrounding district was almost deserted. Inside, however, a voice was speaking, but as I think Parliament was not sitting that day, it probably was the wireless of some caretaker as I only heard it whilst at the rear of the building. There wasn't much to see. I took a snap and, after a wait, boarded a bus back to the Civic Centre where I again called at the office of ANA. Still no news, so I crossed the street to a small modern hotel called the "Civic" and partook of lunch. Calling back at ANA after lunch I learned that I had a seat on the 3.30 so I walked along the few doors to TAA where I had my Canberra/Sydney fare refunded and this cash was passed over again to ANA; the transfer resulting in no extra cost. The Civic Centre, which had been so busy in the morning, was now almost deserted. I lay on the grass in the sun for a while and at 2.45 left in the ANA motor coach which carried us to Fairbairn Airport. After another short wait, the 'plane arrived from Melbourne, was refuelled and we took off at 3.30pm.

The Melbourne/Canberra DC3 had been almost empty, carrying only about half-a-dozen out of a possible twenty-one passengers. This was another DC3, but it was full this time and whereas I had been sitting by myself at a window towards the rear before, I now sat beside a gentleman from Devonport, Tasmania in the very front seat and on the aisle. Shortly after leaving Canberra, the weather began to deteriorate and we were told that it was raining in Sydney. This time we flew at a lower level and by doing so evaded many of the dirty rain clouds, but when nearing Sydney this wasn't possible and soon we were flying 'blind' and coming in on a 'beam'. At approx. 4.40pm, on flashed the sign "No Smoking - Fasten Seat Belts", the operation of the hydraulics was accompanied by a series of 'toots' and we circled in to land at Kingsford-Smith Airport. During the trip we had received tea and biscuits from an extremely courteous hostess who appeared to care for passengers' comfort just as stated in the Airline's pamphlets. ANA is Australia's first airline and a private company. TAA is operated by the Government.

On arrival at Sydney, it was still raining and what-do-you-know - no coat - we hadn't seen rain in a fortnight! Sydney's airport was busier than the others and there seemed to be quite a number of people awaiting the arrival of friends. We boarded our bus and soon covered the 6½ miles to town.

Near the Sydney ANA office is the Wentworth Hotel. There I was told to try Hotel Grand Central (151 Clarence Street) and at this hotel was successful in securing a room for one night. The following morning, however, someone checked out and I spent both nights at this hotel in two different rooms. It was nothing 'Grand', a rather old hotel and just average. The charge was reasonable at 17/- per night for bed and breakfast i.e. approx. 13/8d (69p) sterling.

On arrival I had a wash and shave, cleaned my shoes, had dinner and then out into Sydney. The centre of the city was full of people on the way to participate in their Saturday night's entertainment. Like Melbourne at night, some of the shop windows were lit and other were not. The lighted ones are those having their own power plants as, since the weekly one-day stoppages at the coalmines, the lighting of shop windows from public supplies has ceased. Electric train services have also been curtailed because of these strikes and other restrictions have been imposed such as the imposition of a law forbidding householders to use radios between 8 and 10am each day. The obvious solution to the latter problem is to shut down the radio stations for these two hours, but this is not done as apparently the listeners with portable battery sets have to be catered for.

On Saturday evening, I finished up in the "Trocadero", Sydney's No.1 dance hall. It is a big flashy place where I spent an enjoyable evening. I left the dancing around 10.30pm and walked back to the hotel, purchasing a couple of Sunday 'papers on the way. In Melbourne, incidentally, there is no Sunday 'paper. Everything stops for the weekend and, like Scotland, even the cinemas are closed.

I was out of the hotel by about 9am on Sunday morning. It was a lovely morning and I started off to walk to the famous bridge only about 15 minutes away. At the commencement of the bridge there are many toll entrances through which pass a constant stream of cars. At one side of this, the top level, is the pedestrian crossing and under this level is the railing crossing. At the toll I met a young New Zealand sheep shearer who was also seeing Sydney and who was about to walk across the bridge. I was once going to walk across with him, but decided I couldn't spare the time as there was a lot I wanted to see. From there I walked down towards the quay and was directed there by an ex-Partick man.

Circular Quay is where all the ferries leave from. The Lane Cove Ferry passes under the bridge so I took this one and did the round trip. On returning from this trip, I took the tram from Circular Quay out to the well known Bondi Beach. From Bondi, I returned to Circular Quay and crossed in another ferry to Taronga Park Zoo, reputed to be one of the finest zoos in the world. To make the inspection of the zoo easier, notices recommend that one take the tram to the hilltop and walk down the hill through the zoo. I did this. When coming out of the main entrance at the foot of the hill, I asked a young chap to take a snap of me and it happened he was with his father and mother although I didn't realize this at the time. His father had come out from Crewe, England, 38 years ago with his folks and he was keen to talk just like my father! I returned to Circular Quay with this family who were from Newcastle. The folk here are interested to know of living conditions in the UK, ask if one is here to stay and, upon receiving a negative answer, ask if one would like to come out. The country is full of recent emigrants from Europe and languages of many nations are not infrequently heard. The mother of this family was going to give me their address in case I ever got to Newcastle, but I said there wasn't much chance of my ever being there.

Again at Circular Quay, I boarded another ferry; this time on a longer trip and out to Manly. It was almost dark when I got there, but I saw around the place all right, had tea there, a chat with a business man on the prom', a look in at an aquarium on the prom' and then boarded a bus for a place called St Leonards. There I changed to a train which took me to Milson's Point at the opposite side of the bridge from where I started off and where Sydney's Luna Park is situated. Melbourne also has a Luna Park. They are only large Fun Fairs, but well known places and very popular. Having strolled round Luna Park, without participating in any of the amusements, I crossed in a small motor launch ferry to Circular Quay and caught a tram into the city. And so to the hotel and bed.

Having had breakfast - with two eggs - on Monday morning, I walked down to the shops and purchased postcards and souvenir pictures of Sydney. After that, I walked up and into the Botanic Gardens, but had no time to see them as I had to be at the TAA office by 10.40am when the bus took us out to the airport. The 'plane departed at 11.30am and this time was one of the latest Convairs with seating capacity for forty passengers. The speed of the DC3 is 170/200 mph, whilst that of the Convair is 260/300 mph. The latter carries two airhostesses. This time I was again towards the rear of the 'plane and seated beside a commercial traveller (on his first flight) on the aisle side. Both coming into and departing from Sydney, I did not see the bridge from the air, but as we left we got a grand view of Botany Bay. The Convair flew at 12000 ft and a pilot's log, which was passed round, showed that we were over Albury at 12.48 and flying at 255 mph. I have this log as a souvenir. A light, but tasty lunch was served on the 'plane and at 1.40pm we made a bumpy descent to Essendon Airport. The trips were almost always smooth, but at times, when rain clouds were about, the passage became somewhat bumpy. A coach carried us into Melbourne and I carried on down to the ship. And so ended an expensive, but worthwhile weekend, which cost me in the region of £18 sterling." End of quote.

The flight from Melbourne to Canberra cost A£6-6/- and was made on the Royal Mail Airliner "Todd". The fare from Canberra to Sydney was A£2-15/- and from Sydney to Melbourne A£6-6/-. I returned from Sydney on the Royal Mail Airliner "James Cook" and on 21 March, the (Melbourne) Argus reported: "A Trans-Australia Airlines Convair yesterday broke the speed record on the "rocket" non-stop service from Brisbane to Melbourne by 22 minutes. The [4]Convair, the "James Cook", commanded by Captain J

---

[4] The Convair was the only pressurised aircraft in use on internal flights and ANA described their DC4 Skymasters, which carried forty-four passengers, as 'giants of the air'.

The airfares were reasonable and, as security was not a problem, there was none of the long waits at airports which we suffer today. Transport, to and from city terminals was free. If you were making use of this service, you were requested to be at the terminal fifteen minutes before the advertised time of departure of the coach and, if you were proceeding directly to the airport, fifteen minutes before

Hepburn, flew the 926 miles in 3 hours 26 minutes." The "James Cook" left from Sydney's Kingsford Smith Airport and when I was in the waiting room my name was called over the tannoy. As the previous time I had been called over a tannoy was when crossing the Atlantic on HMT *Queen Elizabeth* at the start of my sea career in July, 1943, it struck me as a coincidence that I was again being called towards the end of it.

---

the departure of the 'plane. The smoking of cigarettes was permitted in all seats, but pipes and cigars were not allowed on the grounds that other passengers objected to strong fumes. Free Personal Travel Insurance cover of £2000 was included in the fare and, at the foot of the Official Flight Log which was passed round the passengers, it said, 'The Captain will be pleased to write you a souvenir copy'. Due to the great distances involved, air travel was expanding in Australia and the airlines were doing all that they could to encourage it. Ansett Airways was another airline in competition on domestic routes. Among the many photographs I took that weekend, was one of the frontage of Sydney's General Post Office in Martin Place. This was because, although I had previously seen boxes labelled City and Other Destinations, the wall of the Sydney GPO had something like fifty boxes carrying the names of various destinations. This method of having senders of letters doing most of the sorting will have gone with the introduction of postcodes and automatic sorting.

Darrell was with me in my cabin when Mr Painter came to inform us that a private showing of 'Western Approaches' was being given at the house of a friend of Kerr's on the evening of Thursday, 15 March. When he said that numbers had to be limited and that only one of us could go, I immediately said that I didn't want to go. He appeared insulted by my reaction, which was due to my opinion of 'Film Star' Kerr, and Darrell went. I have since seen the film more than once on television. Although it was hailed as a great film during the war, it appears dated today.

Melbourne's Luna Park was situated in the district of St Kilda. After Harry and I had a look round the fairground on Saturday afternoon, we had tea before walking almost the whole way back into town and spending the evening at the Trocadero.

As none of my shipmates was interested in going, I went on another Parlorcars coach tour with Mary. This time it was a full day trip to Hepburn Springs, Daylesford and Ballarat and the price, which included lunch, was 30/-. All the tours began at Whight's Tourist Bureau in Flinders Street. We left there at 9am on Sunday, 18 March and returned at 6.30pm. The outward journey was by way of Woodend and Trentham and the inward journey via Ballan and Melton. We had elevenses, consisting of tea, homemade scones and whipped cream, in an old log cabin, lunch in an hotel in Daylesford and afternoon tea in a small country tearoom. At Hepburn Springs we tasted the bubbling active spring water and spent some time in the lovely Botanic Gardens in Ballarat. There we saw the plinth-supported busts of all the Australian Prime Ministers, what were reputed to be the largest begonias in the world and, most surprisingly for me, a statue to the Scottish hero William Wallace. Ballarat, which never seemed to be mentioned at school without linking it with the other gold mining town Bendigo, has gone down in the history books because of the Eureka Stockade of November/December, 1854. A monument commemorates the event when the miners held out against the police because of the imposition of unjust licence fees and other grievances.

Flinders Street is adjacent to the Yarra River (claimed by Australians, due to its muddy appearance, to be the only river in Australia which flows upside down!) and, when the tour ended and we walked along the grassy banks of the river, I had to dive into a lavatory with diarrhoea. The following evening I started shivering as if I had caught a chill and this, together with my upset stomach which lasted for about a week and was most likely due to the amount of spring water I drank, prevented me going ashore again in Melbourne. But I was well content with what I had seen of that fine city, which, with its wide and tree-lined streets, I consider to be one of the most beautiful cities in the world.

The one-day stoppages in the coalfields, referred to in my letter concerning my weekend in Canberra and Sydney, had begun on 5 February. A £2 a week increase in day workers' wages had been refused and when the Coal Industry Tribunal, Mr FH Gallagher, had responded with an offer of £2 a fortnight, if worked without stoppages, the miners in New South Wales, Queensland and Victoria had taken action. This, together with the invalidation of the Communist Party Dissolution Act, resulted in a crisis which brought about a Federal Election on 28 April.

What was described by the (Melbourne) Sun as the 'Communist-dominated' Waterside Workers' Federation was also involved in a pay dispute and, also from 5 February, had operated a ban on overtime work which brought congestion to all Australian ports. But, while this added to the national crisis, it operated in our favour as it gave us more time in port! Due to the Government's fanatical fear of communism, the *Admiral Chase* was being refused Customs clearance at Sydney on the grounds of a rumour that she was being sold for trade with Communist China. The ship, crewed by British officers, was engaged in the Pacific Islands trade. The Master denied the rumour and said that, as it was costing £1000 a day to keep the vessel in port, there would be a claim for demurrage against the Commonwealth.

It was the behaviour of the Melbourne wharfies which drew my attention to Victoria's restrictive licensing laws. There was a break in work, from perhaps 5 till 6pm, and, as the pubs closed at 6pm, they drank as much as they could and returned to the ship half stoned. A wharfie caused an amusing incident concerning the 2nd and 3rd Mates. A big fight in the United States was to be broadcast on the radio that afternoon. The man told Tom Nelson that what we were to hear was only a recording as the fight had actually been fought the previous evening and that 'so and so' had been knocked out in the 3rd round. Armed with this inside information, Tom thought he would have some fun with Peter and bet him that the already defeated boxer would not last beyond the third round. The bet was accepted, we all stood beside the radio listening to the fight and the penny only began to drop when it continued beyond the third round!

The cargo discharged in Melbourne was of a general nature and included the following: in the region of a hundred unpacked and cased saloon cars, cookers, stoves, sewing machines, tiles, machinery, crane parts, glass, screws, bolts, structural steel work, cast iron soil pipes, tipping trucks, earthenware, engines, chemicals, dyes, beds, bales of paper, tissue paper, steel plates and joists, pre-cut timber house sets, carpets, soda ash, tractors, yarns, woollen and cotton goods, drums of cable, salt, potassium nitrate, linoleum, cardboard, felt, cement and fish. Britain was a factory in those days and her ships, flying the Red Ensign, carried her products to all parts of the globe.

Bound for Brisbane, 1233 miles away by sea, we sailed at 3.54pm on Thursday, 22 March, 1951 and passed the *Dolius,* on her way in.

After a fine passage, we anchored off Brisbane on the evening of Monday, 26 March and tied up to a quay in the Brisbane River, in the very heart of the City, at 6.18am the following day. My stomach had continued to bother me and, just when this was getting better, an ulcer developed on my tongue, causing me to speak with a lisp and making every meal an endurance test. But, although continuing to suck potassium chlorate tablets, I was fit to see the sights of Brisbane and went ashore every day. Shortly after we docked, the Agent, Wills, Gilchrist & Sanderson (Pty.) Ltd., brought mail on board. Among my letters was one from of a friend of my mother who had not written for about two years. This lady's letters never contained much more than what the weather had be like in Dundee, but, on this occasion, she gave additional information on deaths and marriages!

Divided by the Brisbane River, Brisbane is known as 'the River City' and five bridges - the Story, the Victoria, the Grey Street, the Indooroopilly Toll and the Indooroopilly Rail - linked the two sides. A sixth bridge, between the West End and St Lucia, had just been approved, but, as we berthed on the city centre side, it was an easy walk into town. I had come to realize that there were no really old buildings in Australia, but it was difficult to grasp that it had been only 127 years since Brisbane had been founded as a penal settlement. Even female convicts had gone about in chains and the factory in which they worked stood on the site of the GPO.

The poinsettia, indigenous to Mexico, is Brisbane's floral emblem and, as the City is sub-tropical, sub-tropical, tropical and temperate region plants, were to be seen everywhere. On the day following our arrival, the temperature was 90°F (32°C), but that was about 7° higher than normal for autumn. Among the City's flowering shrubs and trees were bougainvillea, frangipani, hibiscus and jacaranda. The Botanic Gardens, on the site where officers of the penal settlement once had their gardens, had a small zoo which housed both imported and native animals, including wallabies and kangaroos. I was carrying a bag of mixed nuts and raisins and fed the nuts to a monkey who stuck his hand through the wire mess. When I put a raisin in his hand, he just turned his hand over and dropped it without looking at it. When I gave him a third raisin, to see the reaction, only the mesh restrained him from attacking me.

On the day of our arrival, Denis and I went to see the film 'Annie Gun Your Gun' and thoroughly enjoyed it. Other evenings were spent at the Cloudlands Ballroom which was aptly named because of its elevated position. It was a lovely ballroom and I never came across another in such a beautiful situation from where wonderful views were obtained.

I thought Brisbane's single-decker trams absolutely superb. Made of aluminium and with open windows, the new "R Type" tramcar was claimed to be: 'The first Australian tram with rubber-cushioned wheels; the most streamlined in the world; the second longest street car in service anywhere; fitted with the greatest seating capacity of any street car; the quickest loading and discharging saloon car in service anywhere'. It was a pleasure to travel in them.

A representative of Brisbane Grocery Service visited the ship and gave each of us a list of commodities we could have delivered on board. But, as I had already bought a stack of stuff from Finneys, a similar supplier in Melbourne, I had enough to carry home. And, as this consisted of thirty-seven tins of various items of food plus 1 lb of raisins and 10 lbs of sugar, at 5d a lb, it made up a heavy cardboard box. I had also bought kangaroo bookends and a letter opener made of mulga wood in Melbourne. In the hope of winning a fortune, I bought a share in the Golden Casket Art Union. This lottery, which began for patriotic purposes in 1916, had been run by the Government since 1920 and the money raised was used to fund hospitals and other institutions. A share cost 5/-, but a quarter share could be bought for 1/6d.

On Sunday, 1 April, I took the bus to Mount Coot-tha, which is 750 feet high and from where you can see over Sandgate and the mouth of the Brisbane River to Moreton Bay. I took three snapshots from the viewing platform and later joined them up to give a panoramic view. From Mount Coot-tha, known also as 'One Tree Hill' because a single tree had been left standing when the area had been cleared over a hundred years earlier, I returned to town and took another bus to the Lone Pine Koala Bear Sanctuary, eight miles distant. The zoo had many native birds and animals, but the koalas were the main attraction. A few were munching gum leaves, but most were asleep as the koala sleeps something like eighteen hours a day. I saw the kookaburra in the various zoos and always enjoyed tuning in to the short-wave transmissions of Radio Australia which began with its unique 'laugh'. On the day I visited Mount Coot-tha and Lone Pine, The (Brisbane) Sunday Mail carried the front-page headline 'BRITAIN WILL TRY OUT ATOM IN AUSTRALIA - WOOMERA SITE "IDEAL" '.

The licensing hours in Queensland were much more civilized than those of Victoria and were from 10am till 10pm. Only saloons and licensed hotels could sell alcoholic drinks, but sales were not permitted on Sundays, Good Friday, Anzac Day, Christmas Day and during polling hours on election days. Women were not allowed into saloons and, as all Australian ships were dry, I saw seamen carrying booze back to their ship. In Scotland, at that time, all pubs were closed on Sundays and licensed hotels were permitted to sell drinks only to travellers. This resulted in people 'travelling' on Sundays and a book stating their destination had to be signed. The shop opening hours in Brisbane were from 8.15am to 4.40pm on weekdays and from 8.35am to 11.30am on Saturdays.

I sent an article, comparing life in Australia with that in Britain, to the Brisbane 'Courier-Mail'. When it was returned with the Editor's regrets, I gave it to the Brisbane Telegraph where it met with the same result. One of the things I said in the article was that jobs were easier to come by in Australia and this was indeed the case as the newspapers were full of classified ads. I have heard it claimed that work was easily obtained in post-war Britain, but this was not my experience when I was looking for a shore job a few months later. When I eventually got an office job in the in the autumn, I was paid £6-10/- a week; considerably less than the average Australian male's basic wage of £8-7-6d. I also mentioned that I had seen more drunkenness in Australia than I had ever seen in Britain.

Having discharged cargo similar to that discharged in Melbourne, we sailed for Port Alma at 6.12am on Tuesday, 3 April and arrived there at 3.55pm the following day.

New rates of pay had come into force on 1 March, 1951 so that our salaries now were:

1st Mate	£60
2nd Mate	£47
3rd Mate	£38
4th Mate	£31
2nd Mate	£32
Male Nurse	£27
Chief Steward	£47
2nd Steward	£31-10/-
Chief Engineer	£80
2nd Engineer	£60
3rd Engineer	£47
4th Engineer	£34
1st Radio Officer	*£46

Asst Radio Officer £31
1st Electrician   £50
2nd Electrician   £40

*Plus £6 purser's bonus

Bonuses, 'payable for successful prosecution of voyage', were paid to the Master, 1st and 2nd Mates, Chief and 2nd Engineers and Chief Steward. Holt's rates were above those laid down by the National Maritime Board, but no overtime was paid to officers or petty officers on Company Contract. The NMB rate for an R/O of my experience on a ship of similar class (II) was £40. Holts also gave their officers more leave than the '21 days plus 14 extra in lieu of overtime' laid down by the NMB and full pay, less bonuses, was paid. Also, officers were given a Christmas Bonus of one month's pay on completion of a successful year of trading. All this is why we became Blue Funnel men; loyal to the Company and proud to serve on their fine ships. And the Company did not lose by the fair treatment of their staff. I believe that the high salaries paid to electricians were due to the strength of their trade union, the ETU.

Chinese:
Carpenter	*£24-1/-
Bosun	*£24-1/-
Quarter Master	£20/6/-
No.1 Donkeyman	£15-18-6d
Fireman, Sailor, Asst. Steward,	
Galley Boy, Deck Boy	£14-1/-
No.1 Fireman	*£24-1/-
Ship's Cook	*£23-2-6d
No.1 Leading Stwd	£18-2-6d
Greaser	£14-7-6d

*Plus £2 efficiency bonus

Holiday pay was at the rate of two days' pay per month of service and no allowance was made for Sundays at sea which had been effective for British seamen since April, 1947.

(The new rates of pay for Alfred Holt's British ratings were: Carpenters and Bosuns with over 3 years service - £42 and £40 respectively, Quarter Masters and Firemen - £22-10/-, ABs - £22, Assistant Stewards - £21, Deck Boys - £9.)

At the mouth of Queensland's River Fitzroy (there is another river of the same name in north-west Australia), Port Alma is the deep-water port for Rockhampton. Beside the solitary wharf, which could accommodate only two ships, there were sheds, a canteen for the wharfies, a Custom's hut and a small shop. Farther back from the wharf, were the accommodation huts of the wharfies and a house where women who looked after them stayed. That was all there was to Port Alma and when I have spoken to Australians in subsequent years, they have never heard of the place!

It was only when we were coming alongside, beside the P & O cargo vessel *Perim*, that I remembered it was my father's birthday. I had forgotten to send him a card and when I noticed an old rusting Post Office sign hanging from the ramshackle wharf building, I went down to investigate as soon as the gangway was lowered. A man in shirt sleeves and big soft hat was walking past and when I asked if it were possible to send a cable for here, he replied, "Just a minute till I finish tying up the ship." He was the Postmaster and, due to the time difference, I hoped that the cablegram I sent would arrive home the same day.

We had no cargo to discharge and had come to load gram sorghum. On the day of our arrival, The (Rockhampton) Morning Bulletin reported that a fire in storage sheds at Bajool had destroyed 3500 tons worth £70000, that it was still smouldering and that three firemen were in serious condition at the General Hospital. The article went on to say, 'Although insurance would cover any financial loss Britain would suffer the loss of valuable grain for feeding stock. ....every effort would be made to have sufficient grain sorghum at Port Alma this week to provide a full cargo for a ship (the "Deucalion") due there in the next few days. Apart from grain saved at Bajool there was still some at Port Alma and an attempt would be made to rail the balance needed from western storage centres.' I heard that the shipment of sorghum to Britain was part of a Government scheme and that, after preparation, it was sold at £38 a ton; a hefty price for a farmer to pay. We loaded 20537 bags (1365 tons) of the grain plus a small unbagged quantity; all stowed in No.1 hold.

Campaigning for the forthcoming Federal Election was now in full swing and the front-page headline of The Courier-Mail of 5 April was 'ROWDY REDS SCREAM AT MENZIES'. Robert Menzies, the Prime Minister, had addressed a Liberal Rally in Rockhampton the previous day and, replying to the call of JB Chifley, the Opposition Labour Leader, to get

Australian troops out of Korea, had said that to do this would condone Communist aggression. As in Britain, eighteen-year-old men were being conscripted into the Armed Forces and liable to serve in Korea. Radio station 4RO broadcast Mr Menzies' speech the same evening and I listened to several broadcasts by politicians. At their conclusion, an announcement was made to the effect that the views expressed by a candidate were his own and not those of the station which was 'non political and non sectarian'.

As sea fishing was available, I made use of the line which my grandfather had given me. The best bait was prawn and the wharfies didn't mind us using their nets to catch them. I caught a small perch, which I threw back, and a catfish. A wharfie saw me catch the latter and immediately came over and warned me not to touch it as he said it could inflict a nasty wound. He put his foot on it, removed the hook and it too went back into the sea. When I threw out the line again, I lost the lead sinker and the beautifully plaited leader which my grandfather had made. The weather was hot and one evening when I returned to my cabin, after foolishly leaving the portholes open and the light on, I found it full of a variety of large moths and other insects. I had previously seen preying mantises and had been told that people took them into their houses to rid them of flies.

The wharfies worked only a day shift so that the ship was strangely quiet in the evenings and we had to make our own amusements. Denis produced a housey-housey/bingo set and everyone, including Kerr, took part in games in the saloon. With Denis as an excellent caller, we all enjoyed this diversion to begin with. But we soon became bored with it and a group of us set up a pontoon school in one of our cabins. We played only for pennies, but I found myself winning quite a bit and every time I got an ace and face card and won the bank, I sold it for 3d. After I had done this several times and the holders of the bank had made nothing from it, I won it again. But, when I again offered it for 3d, someone shouted, "Let him keep it this time." They all agreed, no-one would buy it, and, as banker, I *cleaned up*; won about 16/- and my ill-gotten gains funded a trip to Rockhampton!

The trains, which brought our sorghum, came via a bridge over the Fitzroy; right onto the wharf. When I boarded the train, a goods train with one old and grimy carriage at its rear, on the morning of Saturday, 7 April, the only other passengers were the master of the *Perim* and his Agent. I travelled in a compartment with them as far as Bajool, where they got off and were met by a couple in a car. Bajool, about half way between Port Alma and Rockhampton, consisted of only storage sheds and I saw no signs of the fire. Midgee, between Bajool and Rockhampton, and the only other station I saw, was even smaller than Bajool. And, although Rockhampton is only thirty-eight miles from Port Alma, the journey took 3½ hours! This included a long wait in a siding at Bajool to allow a well-laden passenger train to pass on the single track.

Although Rockhampton was the second largest town in Queensland and had one or two fine buildings such as the Post Office on East Street, it reminded me of the towns in the Mid-West I had seen on American films. I was staying overnight, because there was no train back that day. The first two hotels I tried were full, but I got a room at the Leichhardt, an old wooden hotel which had seen better days. The town was so deserted when I walked about in the afternoon, that I asked a woman where everyone was. They were all at the races and fifty per cent of those who were not, were drunk. In the evening, I went to a cinema and saw a film about Scotland called 'The Green Years'. The cinema, which was nicely decorated, was built of tin and the seats were deck chairs. And, sitting drinking coco-cola, I thoroughly enjoyed the film.

The Leichhardt Hotel proved to be excellent and evening dinner, bed and breakfast cost only A14/-. There were no keys for the rooms and every room had a second door leading onto a balcony. The place was scrupulously clean and, for the one and only time, I slept under a mosquito net. I may say that I liked Rockhampton's setting - on the Fitzroy, which was navigable for small vessels, and surrounded by bush-covered hills.

When I went to the railway station to get the morning train back to Port Alma, the Station Master told me that the train was late, he didn't know exactly when it would arrive and to come back in an hour. When it did arrive, he and a boy entered a compartment of the rear passenger carriage and swept it out for me with brooms. Only goods trains ran to Port Alma and as this one had come across the dry bush country carrying sorghum for the ship, it was in a mess. Again I was the only passenger and, perhaps because it was Sunday, there was no shunting into a siding to allow a passenger train to pass. I was back on board for lunch.

That Sunday, 8 April, was census day in Britain so that the following form was completed.

CENSUS 1951

Name of Ship........."Deucalion"
Official No...........144217
In order to assist in the Census of the population the
Master is requested to answer the following questions.-

Please answer "YES" or "NO"

Was the ship in port in the United Kingdom
 at midnight on Sunday, 8th April, 1951?   No
Was a Census Schedule for the ship
completed and delivered or posted to a
Customs Officer or other Enumerator?   No

_____

In a letter to my folks, given to the agent shortly before sailing at 10pm on
Tuesday, 10 April, I said that, after Cairns, our next port-of-call was to be
Djakarta, in Indonesia, and that we expected to anchor at night when
passing through the Great Barrier Reef, as this was the Blue Funnel rule.

The sea was calm and the sun shining as we negotiated a section of the Barrier Reef on our way north. I had not expected to see the Reef itself, but we passed close to islands with lovely sandy beaches and picturesque inlets which are part of it. A Barrier Reef pilot, who was to be with us all the way to Thursday Island at the tip of Cape York Peninsula, had boarded at Brisbane. No doubt because the weather was so good, he kept the ship going throughout the two nights and we tied up to the wharf in Townsville at 7.48am on Thursday, 12 April. The coastal steamer *River Mitta* left that same morning with a cargo of sugar for refineries in the south.

Townsville, spread out over the valley of the Ross River, had only one main thoroughfare. This was wide Flinders Street, which had palm trees and flowers along its centre, and Denis and I browsed round the shops there the following day. When we saw pieces of the coral reef for sale, in various colours, I bought a white piece for 7/6d (37½p). Everywhere we had been, I had tried to get a recording of 'Waltzing Matilda'. I tried again, without success, and left Australia without one.

The town is overlooked by Castle Hill and on Saturday afternoon, Harry and I climbed to the top where a monument to Captain Robert Towns stands. A long winding road led to the summit, but we ignored it and climbed straight up and, although I thought myself fit, this unaccustomed form of exercise took it out of me. But it was worth the effort to get the panoramic view and I again took three photographs which I later joined together. In the distance, we could see the solitary dock which stretched out into the Coral Sea and at which only the *Deucalion* and the *Chanda* lay. The *Chanda* was one of the ships we had spoken to in the Indian Ocean and had arrived that morning to load silver, lead and general cargo for the UK. The locals claim that as Castle Hill is only a few feet short of being classed as a mountain, it is the highest hill in the world!

After returning to the ship for dinner and a clean-up, we joined a gang of lads heading for the Missions to Seamen. There, together with a number of girls and the young padre and his wife, we boarded the Mission bus which took us to the Black River area. This was bush country and it was dark. We lit several fires and a gramophone played as we fried sausages and had a good time in general. And in the bus, on both the outward and homeward journeys, I played the mouth organ while the others sang. I frequently played the mouth organ in those days and a favourite tune around the coast was Bonaparte's Retreat.

Sunday afternoon was spent on Magnetic Island with Darrell, George Thompson, Stewart Wilson, Bill Leitch, Leslie Winthorpe and 'Taffy' Gardiner. The Island, so called because of a lodestone reef, is a favourite playground and locals sometimes spent the weekend there. A fair-sized steam ferry ran between it and the mainland and, as the temperature was in the region of 90°F, we were all about roasted on the way over. Across the entrance of Arcadia inlet, where there was a sandy beach and waving palms, we saw what appeared to a steel net hanging in the water, to afford swimmers protection against sharks.

Almost all the officers attended the Mission Dance that evening and those of the *Chanda* were also there. When I saw a chap wearing glasses, I thought he might be the Sparks, but he proved to be a Dundonian engineer on his first trip to sea.

The *Manunda,* taking passengers on holiday round the coast, tied up beside us on Monday morning. And when we heard that they were holding a dance at Picnic Bay on Magnetic Island that evening, Denis and went on board to see if we could get tickets for those of us who wanted to go. We got the tickets which cost 3/6d and included the price of the ferry.

I went with Harry and although we enjoyed the dance, the others didn't as they landed among a group of obstreperous drunks at the back of the hall. We learned this only afterwards and apparently there had been fights going on in the bar on the floor below. But we had the company of the *Manunda's* drunken crew on the return ferry and it was only the quick action of a ferryman which prevented one of them going over the side when it rolled. I wondered what the *Manunda's* passengers thought of those men in whose care they were.

The *Manunda* had been a hospital ship during the war. She had been in Darwin when the Japanese bombed it in 1942 and a bomb had gone down the funnel, killing ten of the medical staff. And throughout the New Guinea Campaign, she had carried the wounded from Port Moresby to Brisbane. The Blue Funnel *Centaur* was also an Australian Hospital Ship on the same run when she was torpedoed by a Japanese submarine forty miles east of Brisbane at 4.15am on 14 May, 1943. Mercifully, she was on the outward passage so that she carried no wounded, but, of the 333 on board, only one nurse and 63 men were saved; and she was fully illuminated in accordance with the Geneva Convention. The crew were all Blue Funnel men and among those lost was my former Boys' Brigade colleague, Bob Laird, her 3rd R/O. Australia had three hospital ships, the other one being the *Wanganella*.

I had noticed that Joe Birch, our 2nd Steward, had been looking downcast since Port Alma. After going round collecting change for the 'phone, he returned to make me the first recipient of the news that he had just got himself engaged to one of the girls who looked after the wharfies there. Having obtained permission, he flew to Rockhampton, travelled by rail to Port Alma, then spent the weekend with his fiancée and her parents at their farm at Archer. He had met the girl only about three days before we left Port Alma and was now talking about quitting the sea and catching the first boat back to Aussie!

We sailed for Cairns at 6pm on Tuesday, 17 April, 1951 and the *Orestes* (GFPG), which ran between Australia ports and Singapore, was due in to load frozen beef for Singapore the following day.

13 CAIRNS, NORTH QUEENSLAND, AND GOODBYE

AUSTRALIA

As we sailed past Innisfail, about fifty miles south of Cairns, I wondered if Charlie Duncan were there. Charlie had been 3rd Engineer on the *Samite* and, although about thirteen years my senior, we had been buddies during that long and adventurous wartime voyage. His parents were Glaswegians who had made their home in Innisfail and Charlie had been taken there when he was only a year old. But, as he had met and married a girl when his ship was in Glasgow, I doubted if he would return to that small town in Queensland where he had been raised.

We docked in Cairns at 9.36am on Wednesday, 18 April and I received a letter from my father, dated 5 April, saying that he had received my cablegram on his birthday.

The following day a column in the Cairns Post read:

"FILM STAR" CAPTAIN IN CAIRNS - ACTED IN [5] "WESTERN APPROACHES" - NOW MASTER OF DEUCALION - The 9513 ton vessel Deucalion now unloading 400 tons of British steel in Cairns is in charge of a "film star" captain. He is Captain W. K. Kerr, who was the central figure of the British film "Western Approaches" based on convoy work in the North Atlantic during the war. Captain Kerr is also an accomplished water colour artist, who spends much of his spare time at sea painting. On board the Deucalion yesterday he displayed a large number of paintings of subjects ranging from the sea to English landscapes and waterfront scenes. He has completed a series of striking English winter and spring landscapes. Paintings of vessels from the bridge of his own ship are finely executed, particularly one study of a Chinese junk under sail in a heavy wind. Captain Kerr said that the film "Western Approaches" took two years to make and the entire film unit boarded his vessel to film a convoy to the United States. (A section relating filming experiences.) Captain Kerr who is on his first visit to Cairns is a keen †golfer and intends to visit the local links during his stay here. After unloading her steel cargo

---

[5] The radio officer who acted in the film was John Redmond. He had joined Holts in 1939 and left in 1946 to return to his job in the BBC. He became Director of Engineering and was knighted in 1979. †When Kerr had been practising on a beach at Port Alma, he had taken a middy with him to retrieve his balls!

the Deucalion will pick up cargo in Indonesia and return to the United Kingdom via Colombo.

The Cairns Post of Saturday, 21 April carried a front-page photograph of Arbroath Abbey where the Stone of Destiny had been found after a three month search by police. The Townsville Daily Bulletin of Saturday, 14 April had also made the Stone front-page news. "........Thirty Scottish Nationalists early to-day surrounded Forfar police station in Angus, where the historic Coronation Stone was taken after its recovery yesterday. Headed by Miss Wendy Wood, leader of the Scottish Patriots' Association, they demanded to know where the stone lay. But they were too late. Police had shortly before whisked it away to their headquarters in Glasgow. ....The Scottish National Congress has denounced its handing over as a great mistake.... The 3 cwt. stone has been missing from Westminster Abbey since Christmas Day, 1950."

Another item in the Cairns Post read "The Admiralty announced that there was now no reasonable hope of rescuing any survivors from the submarine Affray, missing since she had dived on the night of April 16 with 73 aboard." And during one of the noisiest election meetings held in Cairns, Senator McLeay, Minister for Fuel, Shipping and Transport, had said "Although he had been able to arrange for extra shipping on the North Queensland run, Communist disruption on the southern waterfront was wholly responsible for delays in the service......As a result of this disruption, ships now spent two weeks in port for every one at sea......".

In the UK, ships were discharging and reloading within a month, but, not including the time spent loading in Port Alma, it took seven weeks to discharge the *Deucalion*. And we were to leave Cairns with five tons of cargo remaining on board. But I was not complaining; the delay allowed me to see much more of Australia than I would otherwise have done, The Cairns Post listed the names of all those who had arrived or departed by Australian National Airways, where they were going and where they had come from; an indication that air travel was in its infancy.

I had mentioned to Harry that I used to do my own photographic developing and printing and he had surprised me by coming to my cabin on the day we sailed from Townsville with all the necessary equipment which he had borrowed from another assistant engineer. We had worked in my darkened room until midnight that night, but, as the results were poor, I spent a great deal of Wednesday and Thursday improving on them. On Thursday, we had a walk round Cairns and enjoyed the relaxed atmosphere of the small town where a stray dog attached itself to us and followed us around.

Our cargo for Cairns consisted of a bit more than the steel referred to in the news item about Captain Kerr. No.6 hold contained cases of beer and fish and in No.2 hold there was machinery, linoleum, baths, steel plates, castings and glass-lined tanks. But, as this didn't amount to much, we expected to be away by Saturday afternoon. The wharfies worked till midnight, but, when Saturday arrived and there was only five tons of cargo left to discharge, they refused to work after 5pm. Another hour's work would have completed the job, but they remained adamant. We now knew that our first Indonesian port was to be Macassar and, as we had to be there before the 30th, to pick up cargo covered by April bills of lading, Kerr asked for permission to have our own sailors unload the remaining five tons. When this was refused, he decided to carry it to Macassar. But, as we were not to leave until 6am the next day, this gave us Saturday evening in port.

Fifty Torres Strait Islanders, on their way to Jubilee Celebrations in Brisbane, were giving a dancing performance in Paramatta Park and, as only Nick Robinson, the Middy, was interested in going, I went with him. We went by taxi, which we shared with a young couple and had to insist that we pay our fare as the young man was going to pay the lot. The show began at 8pm and proved excellent. The Islanders, dressed in grass skirts, with bands round their necks and ankles and sometimes wearing masks, looked ferocious indeed. But when they passed us on their way to and from the field, they looked ordinary and intelligent men and they laughed when small children, who showed no fear of them, got in their way. The dances depicted their way of life, particularly fishing, and included war dances. We had never seen any aborigines in the south, but there were many in the audience and they danced and sang along with the Islanders whose musical accompaniment was provided by an elongated drum and a wooden stick beaten on a box.

It is well known now that Australia badly mistreated the [6]aborigines and Nick and I saw an example of this as we walked back to the ship because, having bought programmes and lemonade, I had no Australian money left and Nick had only sixpence. An aborigine was dead drunk and lay on the raised sidewalk beside a line of small shops. He was doing no harm, but a

---

[6] It wasn't until 1967 that aborigines were permitted to become Australian citizens.

white man pulled him to his feet and kicked him on his way. When the aborigine fell down again, the man repeated the performance and I only wish I had had to courage to interfere. Nick bought a pie at a hot dog stand with his sixpence and we halved and ate it as we walked through the town.

We sailed for Macassar at 6.13am on Sunday, 22 April, 1951, rounded Cape York the next evening, and anchored off Thursday Island about 10pm to disembark the pilot who had been with us for almost three weeks. He had brought us safely through approximately 1445 miles of water and the Barrier Reef pilotage is one of the longest in the world. With a "Goodbye lads", he descended a rope ladder into the motor launch which had come out for him and his luggage was lowered after him. He was kind enough to take letters for posting, provided they were stamped and, anticipating this, the wiser ones among us had bought stamps or postage-paid Air Letters in Cairns. The pilot boat was driven by an aborigine and, as we got under weigh again, we watched its lights as it headed towards the bay where a few shore lights twinkled in the distance. Our last link with Australia was broken and I had never had a better time anywhere. It had been a far cry from the continual grind of work on the Far East run where I was responsible for the outward as well as the homeward cargo and where stevedores worked day and night.

14 MACASSAR, SULAWESI (CELEBES), INDONESIA

Our passage was first of all through the Torres Strait, between Australia and New Guinea, then through the Arafura and Sunda Seas to Macassar, 1483 miles from Thursday Island. It had become increasing hotter. We were again in tropical uniform and, as we passed through the shimmering water, we saw smoke issuing from volcanoes on distant islands. In the wireless room, Dutch ships of KPM (Koninklijke Paketvaart-Maatschappij) began to be heard during the day-time but, as soon as darkness came down at about 6pm, static made all communication impossible. I did a bit of dhobying. In such hot weather, whites didn't stay white for long and all my shirts were disintegrating at the same time. The day before we reached Macassar, I celebrated my 26th birthday and stood the customary drinks to my buddies. They all bawled out the 'Happy Birthday' song and George proposed the toast that my hair would grow again because I had had a steward give me a close-cropped haircut. Joe was present, so we made it a double celebration and wished him and his Australian fiancée 'all the best' for the future. There was a piano in the Smoke Room, but nobody played it other than myself and I could play only a few tunes, by ear. The boys knew that I had mastered 'Waltzing Matilda' and when I asked them what they would like, they would obligingly call for 'Waltzing Matilda' and sing heartily as I played it.

When the ship docked at 3.36pm on Saturday, 28 April, 1951, the Agent brought only a few letters, but I was lucky enough to get five. Two of them contained birthday cards and Helen enclosed a book token for 21/- with which I bought the 'Surgeon's Log' by J. Johnston Abraham on my return to the UK. This book was well known to Blue Funnel men as Dr Abraham describes his voyage to the Far East on the Blue Funnel ship *Polyphemus* in 1907. Although he calls the ship *Clytemnestra* and gives the men fictitious names, people knew it was the *Polyphemus*.

There was no cargo for us in Macassar. We were now to set off for Ternate, Bitung and Menado where we were to load copra, the dried oil-yielding kernel of the coconut, before returning to Macassar, via Balik Papan for fuel oil. And, to do the loading, a squad of badjos/labourers was to make the round trip with us. No work was done on Sunday and, on Monday, the remainder of the Cairns' cargo was discharged and the loose sorghum transferred from No.1 hold to a locker in No.6. Also, two motorboats and eight surfboats were winched onto our decks and stores taken on board for the badjos.

Indonesia was in a state of unrest. Force Majeure operated and ships with general cargoes from abroad were undergoing wholesale pillage. The Agent warned us not to go ashore in anything less than groups of four and a curfew existed between about 2 and 5am. The soldiers we saw were all armed, sometimes with Sten guns, and every night we heard the sound of shots. When native prauws neared ships in the harbour, they were fired upon.

I hadn't seen any mosquitoes, but lumps on my thighs testified that they had seen me! I had never before been given anti-malaria tablets, but Denis issued the new paludrine tablets as a precaution. The hot weather had brought out the cockroaches and we had been plagued with them for some time, but now the advance guard of copra bugs arrived from bags piled up on the quay. These black insects, about a quarter of an inch long, were annoying but harmless and, by the time the ship had gone round the islands, it was covered with them. And they remained with us until the end of the voyage.

In the evening, when I tuned across the short-wave band of my radio, I heard Radio Moscow giving the result of the Australian Election which had taken place on 28 April. The Government of Mr Menzies, a coalition of the Liberal and Country parties, had been returned to office with a reduced majority in the House of Representatives. When the counting was completed a few days later, they also had a majority of four in the sixty-seat Senate and, speaking at the declaration of the poll at Kooyong Pool, Mr Menzies said that the Government had been given a specific mandate to resist the inroads of communism.

I was given a copy of the following letter as some of the information it contained concerned me. Menado is not mentioned although we knew it to be on our itinerary.

Macassar, 25th April, 1951

Master m.v. "DEUCALION",
In Port.

Dear Sir,

For your voyage to Ternate and Bitung, the following arrangements have been made.
Motorboats & Surfboats. We are arranging for you to take 2 motorboats (+

or - 6 tons each, with a crew of 3) and 8 surfboats (+ or - 2½ tons each, with a crew of 2) here.

The average consumption of the motorboats is 8 litres Power Kerosene per hour. 11 Drums of Power Kerosene will be supplied by the "Ocean"-wharf and sufficient lubricating oil will be put on board by the N.I.S.E., together with the boats.

All empty drums and remaining Power Kerosene should be discharged on your return at Macassar as all missing drums will be charged to your ship's account at R.50.-- per empty drum.

The surfboats have a standing crew of 2 badjos per boat, while 1 mandoor is in charge of the surfboatmen.

When taking over the motorboats and surfboats from the N.I.S.E., please have an accurate check made of all boatcovers, anchors, etc., as shortage of these on your return will be claimed and charged to your ship's account.

Labour. We have engaged for your vessel 150 badjos, 5 tally-clerks and 17 surfboatmen, as per list attached.

Wages.

Badjos

1 Headmandoor @ R. 150.-- per voyage. (£7-1-6d/£7.7½p)
3 Mandoors   @ R. 4.75 per day.   (4/6d/22½p)
146 Badjos   @ R. 3. 5 per day   (3/6½d/18p)

Tally-clerks:

5 Tally-clerks @ R. 4.75 per day
 (Rate of exchange was Roepiahs 21.20 = £1 sterling.)

Surfboatmen :

 16 Surfboatmen   @ R. 3.75 per day.

Working-hours. The ordinary working-hours are from 07.00 to 12.00 and from 13.00 to 17.00. Kindly arrange for the badjos to have their stores early in the morning (or on the previous night) so as to enable them to cook and finish their breakfast before they start work. Too much time would be lost if the badjos had to stop work for their breakfast.

Overtime. As all shipboard labour are being paid off at this office on the day of their return, you are requested to have separate overtime sheets (in triplicate) ready on arrival at Macassar. These lists should show the total number of men engaged in overtime, the hours worked and amount earned.

Overtime is as follows:-

Badjos   ) Weekdays: before 07.00 between 12.00 - 13.00 and after 17.00
Tally-clerks)   hours at R. 0.60 per man per hour.
Surfboatmen)

Sundays : same overtime hours as weekdays at R. 0.75 per man per hour.

Ordinary working-hours on Sundays or official holidays at R. 0.50 per man per hour.

Motorboats' Crews. These men get a daily premium of R. 0.25 per man, from the day of joining up to and including the day of return.

Overtime.

Weekdays: same overtime hours as badjos.

Sundays :   all day

Holidays   all day

As the overtime for the motorboats' crew varies according to the rank, you are requested to give overtime hours only for each motorboat. Watching motor- and surf-boats at nights when they are in the water is counted as overtime.

Official Holidays. When compiling the overtime lists, kindly note that the 1st, 3rd, 4th, 13th and 14th May are official holidays.

All the shipboard labour have received an advance of wages and no payments should be made to them during their stay on board.

Cigarettes, tobacco, etc. Please note that cigarettes etc. are not to be advanced to the shipboard labour as we are not allowed to settle these through ship's account.

Stores. We are arranging for the following stores to be put on board here. They constitute 26 days' supply for 172 men (badjos, 5 tally-clerks and 17 surfboatmen).

The motorboats' crews are to be fed from the ship's galley. These men are employed by the N.I.S.E. and are considered superior in rank to the badjos. In this connection we request you kindly, if possible, to give them special accommodation as e.g. the hospital cabin or other closed space.

Provisions	Daily Rations	Totals
Rice (beras)	600g per man a day	2685 Kg.
Salted Eggs (telor)	1 egg per man a day	4500 pcs.
Dried Fish (ikan)	128g per man a day	575 Kg.
Green Peas (katjang)	100g per man a day	450 Kg.
Pumpkin (labu)	80g per man a day	358 Kg.
Brown Sugar (gula)	24g per man a day	215 Kg.
Chillies (lombok)	12g per man a day	54 Kg.
Onions (bawang)	10g per man a day	45 Kg.
Blachan (trassi)	3g per man a day	14 Kg.
Tamarind (asam)	10g per man a day	45 Kg.
Salt (garam)	5g per man a day	23 Kg.
Coffee (kopi)	20g per man a day	180 Kg.
Coconut Oil (minjak)	1cl per man a day	45 Ltrs.
Soya (ketjap)	2ml per man a day	9 Ltrs.
Coconuts (klappa)	2pcs. per 100 men	90 pcs.
Firewood		16 M3.

Please note that we have supplied you with double the quantity of sugar and coffee and we request you kindly to issue an extra ration of these at nights when nightwork is done.

With a view to the duration of your voyage we would suggest that you take the following commodities in your vegetable room or refrigerator, viz.: Eggs, Pumpkin, Chillies and Onions. The other stores should be kept in a cool dry place.

Labour Strength. It frequently occurs that after sailing it is discovered that some of the badjos have missed the ship. We request you kindly to ascertain at sea how many are actually on board and to inform us of the exact number, stating also how many badjos failed to join the ship on departure from Ternate and Bitung, were left in hospital, put in jail, etc. This is in order to facilitate calculation of wages at this office.

Empty bags. Empty bags have hitherto been collected in bundles of 10, on the 9 in 1 system. This system however is to be discontinued and you are requested to return the empties once a day in batches of 100. Each batch of 100 should be tallied into a K.P.M. or Copra Fund lighter by a C.F. tally-clerk and a ship's tally-clerk and a receipt issued to the ship immediately upon discharge into the lighter.

Loading Charges. In order to enable us to calculate the loading charges, please provide us with a detailed list, stating separately the quantities of copra loaded with ship's surfboats, Copra Fund lighters, K.P.M. lighters or others and the quantities loaded direct ex coastal vessels.

Badjo- & Stevedoring Gear. These will be supplied by the "Ocean"-wharf as required.

Knives. You will be provided with a supply of knives for the cutting of the copra bags. Please issue these to the Headmandoor only on arrival at loading port and then at the rate of 10 per working hatch, the remainder being kept as spares in case of breakages. They should be returned to the Chief Officer on completion of loading and any discrepancies reported immediately on arrival at Macassar.

Mate's Receipts. M/R's are to be issued in duplicate to the Copra Fund Agent at the port of loading, clearly marked "Original" and "Duplicate". The C.F. Agent will then decide on the quickest means of getting those M/R's to Macassar and you are requested kindly to cooperate with him should it be required to despatch them by your vessel. It is further requested that only one collective M/R be issued for the copra loaded for one destination and being one parcel. Two copies of the M/R's to be handed to us upon arrival at Macassar. We are supplying the Chief Officer with blank M/R's. Examples of how the M/R's should be made up are shown in the "Instruction Folder" under the heading "General".

Bags lost overboard. In the event of bags of copra accidentally falling out of the slings into the water, you are requested to issue an affidavit, setting forth exactly what took place. Of these affidavits the C.F. at loading port require the original plus 2 copies, ship's Agents 1 copy and 1 copy should be handed to us upon arrival at Macassar. Please note that in order to recover claims on lost bags from the Insurance Co., it is essential that the affidavit should expressly mention that the loss occurred through circumstances beyond human control and all responsibility on the part of the ship or crew be refused on those grounds.

Despatch. In order to ensure an efficient despatch of the surfboats we suggest that one or two responsible officers be put in charge of transport in the roads. They should be the only men from whom the coxswains of the motorboats receive orders. As the motorboats' native crew cannot be relied upon we would suggest that you appoint one ship's engineer to supervise the upkeep etc. It has already happened several times that the native engineers omitted to lubricate the engines, which naturally resulted in breakdowns. Much time has been lost in loading the surfboats when after arrival ashore the slings have not been prepared beforehand. The surfboatmen should make the slings ready when returning ashore with empty boats. The headmandoor has already received instructions to this effect but we request you remind him of this should it prove necessary.

Guestwarps. Please note that it is of the utmost importance that a guestwarp be rigged round the whole length of the ship. This is in order to facilitate the movements of the loading craft and the motorboats. This guestwarp should be on the water-level.

Reports. Messrs. Alfred Holt & Co., Liverpool, will be most interested in detailed reports of the copra loading. We should be very grateful if you would supply us with a copy of those reports.

Copy loading Equipment Macassar. Kindly be referred to copy of a letter from Messrs. *N.S.M. "Oceaan", Amsterdam, dd. 23/6/49, under this heading, which has been inserted in the "Instruction Folder" section "General".

Telegraphic Communication. It is requested that you keep us well advised of the following:- 1) Arrival at Ternate. 2) Quantity of copra loaded each day. 3) ETD Ternate ETA Bitung. 4) ETD Bitung ETA Macassar.

Yours faithfully,
MacLaine, Watson & Co. N.V.
(Scrawled initials) Agent.
Agents:- *OCEAN S.S. CO., LTD.

*Alfred Holt & Co.'s Blue Funnel Line comprised Ocean Steam Ship Co. Ltd., China Mutual Steam Navigation Co. and Nederlandsche Stoomvaart Maatschappij "Oceaan" N.V.; the latter known as Dutch Blue Funnel.

The first ten names on the list given to me by the Agent were:

No.	Name	From
1	Makkattang - Headmandoor	Mamadjang
2	Adji - Mandoor	Marijo
3	Bota - Mandoor	Mamadjang
4	Roppa – Mandoor	B. Lompowa
5	Rumpa	Maritjaja
6	Emba	Kp.Parang
7	Djapa	Mamadjang
8	Nunggio	Mamadjang
9	Undjung	Mario
10	Ali	Mamadjang

With badjos milling about everywhere, we sailed for Ternate at 3.48pm on Wednesday, 2 May, 1951.

With Mrs. Leigh, Indian Ocean.

Immigration, Port Phillip Bay, Victoria. Mr. Kirk
standing (glasses) and Ixion in the background.

Portrait of Helen, received in Williamstown.

Denis and me, Test Match, Melbourne.

Spectators invade the pitch at end of Fifth Test Match, Melbourne.

Harry Watson (white shirt), St Leger Stakes, Flemington Racecourse, Melbourne.

With Darrell, Melbourne.

At Australian National War Memorial, Canberra.

On Lanecove Ferry, Sydney.

Toll points, southern end, Sydney Harbour Bridge.

Taronga Park Zoo, Sydney.

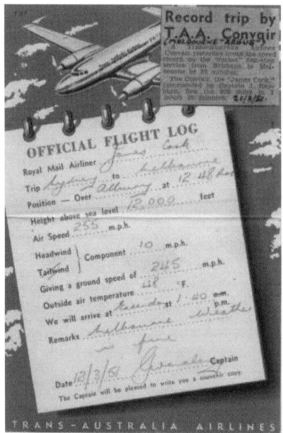

Flight Log.

With Mary Bowring, Observation Point, Mount Dandenong.

Tramcar, Adelaide Street, Brisbane.

Viewing point, Mount Coot-tha, overlooking Brisbane.

Rockhampton Railway Station.

With Darrell, Great Barrier Reef.

Deucalion, Townsville.

In Flinder's Street, Townsville.

View from Castle Hill, Townsville.

Leaving Magnetic Island Ferry, Townsville.

S. Wilson, W. Leitch, D. O'Byrne, G. Thompson, L. Winthorpe and H.
Gardiner, Magnetic Island Ferry.

"FILM STAR" CAPTAIN IN CAIRNS

ACTED IN "WESTERN APPROACHES"

NOW MASTER OF DEUCALION

The 9513 ton vessel Deucalion now unloading 400 tons of British steel in Cairns is in the charge of a "film star" captain. He is Captain W. K. Kerr, who was the central figure of the British film "Western Approaches" based on convoy work in the North Atlantic during the war.

Captain Kerr is also an accomplished water colour artist, who spends much of his spare time at sea painting. On board the Deucalion yesterday he displayed a large number of paintings of subjects ranging from the sea to English landscapes and waterfront scenes.

He has completed a series of striking English winter and spring landscapes. Paintings of vessels from the bridge of his own ship are finely executed, particularly one study of a Chinese junk under sail in a heavy wind.

FILMED ON CONVOY SHIP

Captain Kerr said that the film "Western Approaches" took two years to make and the entire film unit boarded his vessel to film a convoy to the United States. Relating humourous incidents during the "film voyage," Captain Kerr said that the movie people were a "crazy outfit."

He added that some distance at sea during the journey he was in his bunk when he heard a commotion on the deck and went out to see a nearby tanker ablaze close to his vessel. His ship was loaded with ammunition and was positioned in the centre of the convoy for safety.

The film director was bewailing the fact that cameras were not set up to "shoot" the tanker and made a request that they should turn round and sail close into the tanker to take "shots through the flames."

Captain Kerr said that the ship could have blown up at any time where she was and a refusal was hardly necessary.

Part of article in Cairn's Post.

Souvenir programme.

Badjoes boarding, Macassar.

Lowering surfboat, Ternate.

Tally clerk receiving counting stick, Ternate.

Loading a surfboat, Ternate.

Laden surfboat being towed to ship, Ternate.

Darrell and me with tally clerks, Ternate.

With locals, Ternate.

On the pier, Ternate.

73

With Peter Overend at entrance to disused cinema, Ternate.

With local girls, Ternate.

Ternate taxi.

Bananas and coconuts.

Boat which brought me to the shore, Bitung.

Bitung.

Labourers and clerks, Bitung.

Badjoes complete loading No.2 hold, Menado.

With Harry at war memorial, Menado.

Mr. Dreesman's launch returns towing prauw with cargo mail, Menado.

Manioc meal being loaded from barge, Java.

Dhobying at sea, Indonesia.

Deucalion in the lock at Ijmuiden, enroute to Amsterdam.

Lynas pilot boat.

Joe Birch, me and 'Taffy' Gardiner, sailing up the Mersey.

With Harry, Bromborough.

At Festival of Britain.

Eric, Mother, Dad and me, Festival of Britain.

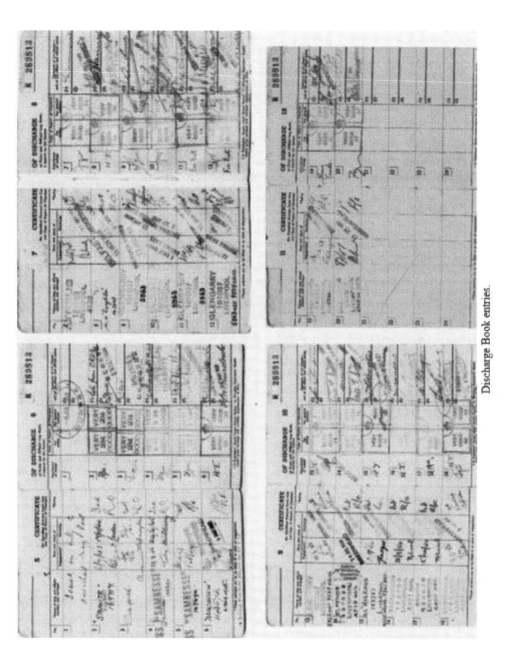

Discharge Book entries.

83

At entrance to Portishead Radio Station, Highbridge, Somerset.

It was 755 miles to Ternate (pronounced Ternaté) taking the southern route round Sulawesi and by way of the Molucca Sea and Pitt Passage, between the islands of Buru and Sanana. We were dubious about the badjos and had been warned not to leave our doors unlocked or portholes open when we left our cabins. No provision was made for the badjos comfort. Their quarters were directly below us in the main deck housing and they had the use of the top of No.4 hatch. At either side of the hatch were two large metal fireplaces with NSMO Makassar stamped on them. Beside these were piles of firewood and this was where their cooking was done. But as the badjos were dirty smelling thieves, they inspired little sympathy and we soon learned that we had to keep our doors and portholes closed even while we slept.

Ternate is a small volcanic island in the Moluccas (Maluku). Its circumference at the shoreline is only six miles and its summit 5400 feet above sea level. The twin-peaked dormant volcano had suffered severe and destructive eruptions in the past; the worse occurring in 1763 and the last in 1909. And, as it lies in position 0°40'N 127°30'E, it is close to the equator, which we crossed to reach it. I stood at the port rail as we moved round to the anchorage. The luxuriant vegetation included coconut palms and banana trees and, set in the clear calm water, it looked a tropical paradise. The *Deucalion* was too large to go alongside the old and rickety wooden pier so that we anchored in the harbour at 9.18am on Saturday, 5 May.

The view from the ship was idyllic. The harbour itself was beautiful and we could see the small island of Tidore, only a few miles to the south, and the large island of Halmahera, 14 miles to the east. Close to the sandy beach were two large aluminium or zinc godowns (the name for a warehouse in the East) on which was painted in large letters JAJASAN KOPRA (COPRA FUND). And, to the right of the godowns, were a few small buildings and the pier from which a dusty road led along the shore to the village.

Work commenced right away. The motorboats and surfboats were lowered into the water and were soon on their way to collect the copra stored in the godowns. A motorboat could pull several empty surfboats, but only one loaded one. But this was sufficient as surfboats, not being pulled, were either being loaded or unloaded.

The system was primitive, but efficient. Local coolies carried the bags of copra from a godown, across the beach, to the water. As each coolie left the godown, a tally-clerk handed him a short stick. Thirty yards farther on, another tally-clerk collected the stick and this indicated the number of bags loaded into a surfboat. The coolie then waded out to the surfboat and the men in the boat used hooks to pull the bag on board, onto a rope sling stretched across the boat's floor. When the surfboat was fully loaded, a motorboat towed it out to the ship where the sling was brought on board by a winched derrick and lowered into a hold. The badjos down the hold then slit open the sewn ends of the bags, emptied them and then used their shovels to spread the copra.

It soon became evident that the main objective of the badjos was to steal the jute bags in which the copra was carried, plus anything else they could lay their hands on. Each bag was worth Rs.10 to them, about 2½ times their daily rate of pay, and the prevention of theft became a major concern. They secreted the bags absolutely everywhere and the mates had the constant task of searching the ship for them. At night, acetylene flares could be seen all round the ship. The flares became brighter as the prauws on which they were burning approached, then went out as the prauws came closer to our bow or stern. And the badjos would be there to lower bags into them. As there was no law and order and the thieving so prevalent, it was impossible to punish a thief, even when caught in the act. When the badjo's quarters were searched, they stood by as bags were retrieved from under their makeshift beds! Towards the beginning of our stay, when everyone was suspected, I was supplied with a metal counter to check on the shore tally-clerks who operated the stick method of counting, but I found their counting to be correct.

The mates, who had the brunt of the pressure, were soon complaining about the lack of co-operation received from the Radio Department and relations between us became so strained that Peter and Mr Painter barely spoke to me. But they were under extreme pressure as, in addition to their hazardous and tiring cargo work, Kerr had them maintaining normal sea-watches. The latter also applied to the engineers, but they were not called upon to do extra duties. The midshipmen were, of course, also involved and Kerr even enlisted Denis to keep security watches although this was well outside his province as a nurse. Strangely enough, I could see that Denis enjoyed this as he strutted round the decks like a young lad, but it didn't take long for his enthusiasm to wane.

The most dangerous work undertaken by the mates was seeing that the trimming was done properly. To do this, they had to go down the holds among the badjos, make a space in the copra and crawl under the coaming. On one occasion, a shovel narrowly missed Tom Nelson as his head was emerging. A show of fearlessness was essential and Tom displayed this. It was not uncommon for the mates to have copra thrown at their backs and when this happened to Tom, he picked up a piece and landed it squarely on a badjo's nose. Fortunately, this just brought roars of laughter from the other badjos. Only a minority of them was vicious.

Every morning, Darrell and I went ashore to supervise the counting of the returned empty bags. One of us went ahead of the empty-bag convoy to see that the empties were properly discharged on arrival at the beach, while the other landed at the pier and walked round to the godown. I enjoyed these trips as the locals were friendly. I have a snapshot of myself on the pier with a happy group of youngsters and a heron they had caught, and another of Darrell and me with some of the tally-clerks. The men, who did the counting of the empties, called out the numbers - satu, dua, tiga, etc. - and, when they got to sapulu (ten), they shouted it loudly and laughed. As no-one knew a word of English, we soon learned the numbers and a few useful [7]phrases. Thousands of bags were counted each day, but of the total of 43043 counted out of the godown, only 42128 empties were returned; a deficit of 915, worth about £218!

We took swimming trunks ashore with us and, when the counting was finished in the afternoon, we went swimming from the lovely beach, a couple of hundred yards from where the surfboats were loading. Engineers joined us in the sport and it was a pleasure to swim in the clear warm water. But, when we were returning to the ship by launch one afternoon, I saw Kerr standing on his bridge deck with binoculars slung round his neck. As we neared the ship, he indicated to me to come up to him and I could see, even at a distance, that he was seething with anger. I climbed the stairs in trepidation and never was confronted by such an angry man. He railed at me for swimming when I 'should have been counting bags', threatened to put me in irons and to have Darrell and me trimming copra down the holds with the badjos! He was so possessed of anger that there was no opportunity to explain that the bags had all been counted. He didn't want to know and put a stop to anyone swimming from then on. No-one was

---

[7] Although the official language of Indonesia is Bahasa Indonesia, Ternate has its own language, written in Arabic script. It was the first part of the Moluccas to accept Islam, but some islanders are Christians.

going to enjoy themselves at Ternate. Kerr had, of course, seen us through his binoculars which he was using to keep his eye on the boats going to and from the shore. And by doing this, he learned that the surfboatmen were emptying full bags of copra into the sea and stowing the empties in the boats! After dinner that evening, we saw an enormous ray in the water and wondered at the wisdom of swimming!

I walked up to the village a couple of times where the people were friendly and seemed to enjoy being photographed. It was a ramshackle place with some broken-down empty houses which I suspect had once been occupied by the Dutch and which had steep protruding roofs to shed the heavy downpours prevalent in the tropics. Prior to the breakdown in our relations, I went to the village with Peter and we had our photograph taken outside the dilapidated-looking picture house called the Columbia Theatre. I was able to buy a film for my camera in a native shop. It cost the exorbitant price of Rs.15, but, as this was what we got from selling a tin of Players Cigarettes, it actually cost me 1/9d (9p). We were all dealing in cigarettes and I was amassing capital with which to buy a pair of Bali Heads if and when the opportunity arose. As souvenirs, I bought a small sewing basket, said to have been woven on Halmahera, and collected a small interesting shell, which proved to be a Murex Haustellum or Snipe's Bill, from the beach.

Coconuts and bananas were plentiful and cheap and one of the shore mandoors sold me two stalks of bananas. These were of some weight and awkward to carry, but, when I made to lift a stalk, he signed that he would have them brought on board. As there was something like six bunches on each stalk, this was a lot of bananas. And, as they went bad quickly, my pals and I didn't allow this to happen!

We sailed at 7.36pm on Saturday, 12 May and only one small KPM vessel, which tied up at the pier, had made a brief call during our stay.

Postscript: The first Europeans to come to Ternate were the Portuguese. They arrived in 1512, but were expelled by the natives in 1574. When Francis Drake visited Ternate and other Spice Islands during his 1579-1580 circumnavigation of the world, his ships loaded cloves and the Sultan of Ternate granted the monopoly of cloves to the English. But by the time English ships arrived in 1604, the Sultans of Ternate and Tidore were unable to provide them with cloves as they had been forced to sell them to the Dutch. In 1606, the son of the Sultan of Ternate, who had promised the cloves to the English, granted the Dutch a spice monopoly and subsequently became a vassal of the Dutch East India Company. Both he and the Sultan of Tidore wrote letters of apology to James I and VI explaining why they had been unable to keep their promise and asking his pardon. But, due to the restriction of clove production in the 17th Century in order to maintain high prices, revolts occurred which brought an end to their production in the northern Moluccas.

It had always been believed that clove and nutmeg trees could grow only in the Moluccas, but this was disproved by Pierre Le Poivre so that they now grow in various parts of the world. The story of how he did this is one of high adventure, but it is sufficient to say here that, during the second half of the 18th Century, he had clove and nutmeg plants brought to the Ile de France (Mauritius) where he was Intendant/Colonial Official. The plants were successfully cultivated in his own botanical garden and then distributed to other French colonies such as Cayenne, in French Guiana, and islands in the West Indies. The original source of the nutmeg was the central islands of the Moluccas and the Islands of Pemba and Zanzibar, in Tanzania, are now the greatest producers of cloves. Incidentally, the French word for pepper is not derived from the name of the Frenchman.

Having crossed the Molucca Sea during the night, we anchored in the fine natural harbour of Bitung, on the eastern side of the northern tip of Sulawesi, at 8.24am on Sunday morning. Again we looked upon a palm-fringed shore and could see the bamboo huts of the village. The motorboats and surfboats were lowered and the same procedure of loading copra was resumed.

MacLaine, Watson & Co. N.V. had an office in Menado and Mr Dreesman drove across from there in a jeep. Although a few Europeans and Euro-Asians lived on Ternate, we had not seen any of them and none had any connection with our business. Mr Dreesman was therefore the first European to board the ship since Macassar. I found him an extremely nice man and he told me something of his history. He had first come to the then Dutch East Indies, twenty-five years previously and, in those days, had liked the country very much. When the Second World War broke out, he was an officer in the Dutch Air Force and was captured when the Japanese took the Indies. After a year in Java, he was shipped to Siam where he spent a further three years as a prisoner of war and where he was ill most of the time; suffering from malaria, dysentery and tropical sores. Regarding the sores, he said that they had been cleared up in a most remarkable way. The Dutch doctors had no medical supplies, but one doctor had prescribed that he should sit in a certain stream. He did this every day and little fish came and sucked the pus out of the sores until he was eventually cleansed. The news that the war had ended came as a complete surprise as the only news they received came from the Japanese censored Siamese press. And, due to illness and the fact that they got little else that a small quantity of rice each day, he was incapable of using his legs. He eventually returned to the Indies to look for his wife and found her working in an army canteen in Batavia (now Djakarta).

Mr Dreesman appeared to be in his late forties and when I asked him how he liked Indonesia now, he just shook his head and said, "Terrible, but what can I do? When I was home, I tried to get a job there, but could get nothing worthwhile. I have only worked out here and I'll just have to put up with it." He considered that the country was heading for ruin and reckoned that the present state of affairs could go on for only another five years. "Do you think they'll ask the Dutch to come back?" I asked. "Yes," he replied, "but I don't think they'll come. I think the Americans will step in and then they (the Indonesians) will know all about it."

There was ample evidence that the country was on the verge of anarchy and foreign-owned tea estates and rubber and sugar plantations were facing a crisis in spite of the high prices being paid for their produce. Independence had resulted in such a display of hatred against the Dutch that sugarcane was being regularly destroyed in eastern Java. Because of banditry and lack of police protection, some plantations had already been abandoned while others could be approached only during daylight hours. And those that were worked were beset by labour troubles. It is little wonder that the young Dutch agent at Macassar had expressed the opinion that Indonesia would probably turn to communism.

None of this hatred was, however, shown to us by the local people. Leaving Darrell to do the counting of the bags one morning, I had a walk through the village with my camera. On either side of the wide earthen road were what appeared to be deserted houses which I thought may have once been occupied by Dutch families. These houses all had thatched roofs and were raised on concrete blocks to afford protection against predators such as lizards and snakes. When the motorboat landed me at the beach, I would have had to jump out into the water, but a young man immediately presented his back to me and gave me a piggyback ashore. I took a couple of pictures of groups of tally-clerks and labourers and was given the same service when I returned to the boat.

My clerical work now included typing the affidavits referred to in the instructions provided by MacLaine, Watson under the heading Bags Lost Overboard. An affidavit had to be made out when (full) bags fell out of a sling (into the water) and when it was an accident beyond human control. I never saw so many accidents beyond human control, although Kerr preferred to use the term Act of God, and the theft of empty bags continued at an even greater pace.

The badjos profited from their slow and indifferent labours by working overtime every day. Mr Painter gave me a note of the hours and it was left to me to work out the total cost in man-hours, taking into account Sundays and recognized holidays. Examples from the sheets I typed were:

DATE	DAY	TERNATE TIMES	HRS	NO.MEN	BADJOS' OVERTIME	ROEPIAHS
5.5.51	Sat.	5 - 8pm	3	140	420 HRS@ R. 0.60	252.00
6.5.51	Sun.	7am-12am	5	140	700 HRS@ R. 0.50	350.00
6.5.51	Sun.	1pm-5pm	4	140	560 HRS@ R. 0.50	280.00
6.5.51	Sun.	5 - 6pm	1	140	140 HRS@ R. 0.75	105.00

This continued until the day we left Ternate when the total cost of overtime amounted to Rs.3087. At Bitung, it came to Rs.2342.70 and, eventually, at Menado, Rs.2239.95. Separate lists were made out for the Tally-clerks and Surfboatmen. The motorboats were named AMSTERDAM I and II and the motorboatmen's total overtime given as follows:

AMSTERDAM I - TOTAL OF 580 MAN HOURS TO BE DIVIDED AS REQUIRED. AMSTERDAM II - TOTAL OF 577 MAN HOURS TO BE DIVIDED AS REQUIRED.

As some of the badjos had deserted at Ternate, the number shown on the sheet was reduced to 137 in Bitung. But, although the same number was shown again on the Menado list, we knew that more had deserted at Bitung and Menado, but had no way of ascertaining the exact number.

I calculated the tonnage of copra loaded daily into each of our six holds. Although a bag could weigh anything between 70 and 74 kilograms, I took 70 kilograms for my calculations, converted this to pounds avoirdupois and then into tons. We loaded 2952.6 tons at Ternate, 984.2 at Bitung and 1476.3 at Menado. And for the one and only time in my life, I found a practical use for logarithms.

We sailed from Bitung at 9.12pm on Tuesday, 15 May, rounded the northern tip of Sulawesi during the night, and anchored off Menado at 9.24am the next morning.

Menado, on the coastal plain at the foot of Mount Klabat, was a town of only about 28000 inhabitants although today it is nearing the 400000 mark. Harry, Joe and I went ashore on the afternoon of Friday, 18 May and, being Europeans, encountered the usual curiosity. The shops were all of the bazaar open-fronted type, owned by Chinese, Malays and Indians e.g. 'Toko Bombay Besar' (big), where we were met with the courtesy I generally experienced in the East. I had saved one hundred roepiahs from the sale of cigarettes, but as the Bali Heads which I saw were poor, I decided to wait till Java. I did, however, buy two beautifully made silver filigree brooches of floral design; one for Helen and one for my mother.

We were again at anchor in the harbour and Mr Dreesman regularly came out to the ship by motor launch. One day, he brought his wife. She was an exceedingly fat lady and as she climbed the gangway, the badjos all howled at her in derision. We all thought the display disgraceful and felt for the lady. But, in such a tense atmosphere, with the badjos barely obeying orders, there was nothing we could do about it.

In an attempt to speed up the work, lighters, as well as our surfboats, brought out the bags of copra, but the badjos were still more interested in thieving than in working. Indeed, they disliked the trimming so much that work was almost at a standstill and, when there was still 700 tons to load, Kerr wired Djakarta for permission to sail for Balik Papan and have the trimming completed in Macassar. But this was not allowed.

Work generally started about 7.30am and continued until anything between 4.30 and 5.30pm. Heavy rain stopped work at 2.30pm on Thursday and there was no loading on Sunday to allow the badjos to catch up with the trimming. As I was now otherwise engaged, Darrell was supervising the counting of the empties on his own, but as the counting was done by representatives of the Jajasan Copra Fund who didn't come on board as promised, Darrell got the Sunday off. Just after dinner that day, the wind rose to such an extent that it was feared that our anchors would drag and allow us to drift towards the shore. Kerr decided it was safer to head out to sea, but as one of the anchors was being raised, it parted from its cable and plunged back into the water. The sea was calm, but it was dark and raining heavily as, under a cluster of lights, Mr Painter supervised Chinese sailors rigging a spare anchor. We spent the night cruising back and forth in the bay. Intermittent rain delayed loading on Tuesday, but it was completed the following morning, and bales of crepe rubber had also been loaded.

Mr Dreesman paid us a last visit just before we weighed anchor and I stood on deck watching his departing launch as we began to move ahead slowly. And it was already in the distance when I saw it approach a prauw and turn back to the ship with the prauw in tow. As it neared the ship, Mr Dreesman called out to me that the prauw had cargo mail for us and I raced up to the bridge to inform Kerr who had not seen what was happening. He stopped the ship and the mail was brought up the gangway.

With 5413.1 tons of copra and a quantity of empties still on board, we sailed for Balik Papan at 11.42am on Wednesday, 23 May. The theft of empty bags had reached its peak in Bitung, but was still significant in Menado. When those remaining on board were finally counted, it was learned that, out of the total of 78372 bags delivered to the ship, only 73542 had been returned: a deficit of 4830.

During the passage through the Celebes Sea and Macassar Strait to Balik Papan, Kerr made out his required report. I typed it out and it read:

m.v. "DEUCALION" VOYAGE 64
MAY, 1951
REPORT ON MACASSAR BADJOS

Our quota was 146 with 5 tallyclerks and 16 surfboatmen and 4 mandoors. It is a pity these men cannot be screened before boarding. We refused one with contagious skin disease and found after sailing that we had a lunatic and four sick men who never did any work for 3 weeks except perhaps steal. They were the most objectionable, despicable, dirty, verminous, lawless mob of thieves and cut-throats and other things ever to board a ship. They even fouled their quarters. The mandoors were incapable of getting them to understand work - they didn't come on board to work - not with an empty sack racket prevailing at all the out ports.

First night out, the C/O (Chief Officer/1st Mate) had a nocturnal visitor through his port into his room whilst asleep and he lost several garments. Chinese forecastle was entered and gear lost. Stewards reported thefts. The 2nd day it was obvious that strongest precautions were necessary - officers' port windows were barricaded with 2"x2", and sleeping with shut doors in the tropics can be imagined. The steel doors between 3 and 4 T.D. (Tween Deck) were forced - forecabin locker door was forced, steel padlocks were no deterrent to these gentry. It was nothing to their ultimate aim - the sack stealing. In Ternate it was evident that a flourishing business was afoot - day and night continuously my officers (mates) and middies and male nurse were on patrol, unearthing sacks from every conceivable quarter, in the copra below hatches, on deck under winches, bundles neatly tied and buried for removal - ceaseless and untiring the search went on and always fruitful - hiding places were denuded and found to contain more again in a few minutes time. We had to avoid "incidents" - this was paramount, as instructed, and the coolies knew it. It appeared that the sacks were their lawful loot - at 10 guilders (the Dutch equivalent of roepiahs) per sack ashore they were not interested in work. Surfboatmen were seen dumping copra enroute to ship and keeping the sack and in this respect our tallymen were worse than useless, cooking tallysheets and in collusion with badjos. They'd tally 100 every boat irrespective of what it contained, and the surfboat which dumped copra (as seen by me from my deck with glasses) was checked by me and found to have 98 bags - tallymen had already tallied 100 before it was discharged. Such widespread unutterable skulduggery was appalling. The tally by copra fund ashore is foolproof - surfboatmen were the biggest offenders - the go-betweens, inexperienced, not boatmen but expert thieves. They don't know the end from a bight of rope, the rudder was a toy to be played with and as for boatmanship - there wasn't any and after hours of explaining right ways and wrong ways they were unchanged. First day at Ternate, one lost his rudder and two hooks. No.1 motorboat got ashore stern first and damaged propeller and shafting and his engine has a knock - our engineers kept him working and they say his engine is in a bad way and needs new rings and an overhaul.

At Bitung the sack "business" was even worse. I called for military security to keep local prauws away and after the military "heads" had been refreshed they promised me a boat patrol. At 12.30am my 2nd Mate informed me that the boat patrol was supervising illicit transferring of empty sacks from aft. This is the port where the C/O was stoned by the locals when he was searching surfboats - he was interfering with the combine but managed to collect 100 sacks. All officers (mates) by this time were on continuous watches day and night - loading became of secondary importance to badjos, and about this time trimming was more urgent than ever. This was the most hateful job with the badjos. Could we or the mandoors get them to trim? They'd sneak off anywhere, a tired lot, except when keeping a sack "assignation" in the night - all night long they'd be found in holes and corners loitering with intent. I never knew that such lawlessness prevailed anywhere. Patient, never ending effort to steal, and a patient never ending effort on our part to prevent it. Our night vigils and searches averaged over 150 sacks nightly, sometimes many more, and always dangerous work as these badjos resented the idea of being denuded of their spoils. My officers suffered minor assaults but mechanically carried on in the face of opposition and threats. Mandoors and all were in the "business" and quite hopeless, and when questioned knew nothing. They used to shout and exhort the badjos, but that was only a gesture. The trimming was the snag - full bags were buried to "bolster" up the appearance and officers were busy "sounding" for them when not otherwise engaged. My 2nd Officer, emerging from below the hatch coamings, from one of these "forays", had a steel trimming shovel thrown at his head. Had this hit him, there might have been dire consequences on both sides. The military in all ports were quite useless - not worth their salt - indeed, with their request for free cigarettes and food and rooms to sleep in, and aiding and abetting and protecting thieves, they are best left out of consideration. The whole venture has been a nightmare for everybody - a ceaseless vigilance against theft of personal property and ship's gear and cargo. Gone are the willing and quiet coolies of Java and in their place we have organised lawlessness and nationwide crime.

I commend my [8]officers and male nurse and midshipmen in the completion of a most heartbreaking job working with those animals who are disguised at badjos and board the ship for one purpose, namely, to plunder.

SIGNED (Wm K Kerr)
MASTER
m.v. "DEUCALION"

In his LOADING REPORT AND REPORT ON MACASSAR BADJOS, Mr Painter used my bag and tonnage calculations then went on to say:

It may be noted from the figures on the previous page that the initial loading rate bears but little proportion to the final loading rate. Whereas, upon opening up another hold space to the badjos (as on the 14th and 15th of May) the loading rate is improved, it all must needs, at the final loading, be reduced to poor figures. This is due to the trimming problem, badjos hate trimming, for every ten men sent to trim, three will work desultory whilst the others dodge, sleep or sit on their shovels. The shovels are poor and many handles were in bad condition upon receipt. These soon became broken and useless. Fifty per cent of them ought to be of the sturdy 'pick shovel' type as used generally in Malaya. These would stand up to the work better, be more adaptable to the 'Eastern muscle type of working' and would be less of a hazard to the ship's officers all of which had the ordinary type thrown at them, spear fashion, as they emerged in difficult belly crawling attitudes from the holds whilst supervising the trimming. No provocation was given at any time to the labour beyond discouraging them to build 'fake' bulkheads, which they are prone to do at any and every opportunity. On the whole, the badjos worked poorly, work being a secondary consideration to that of stealing for which reason alone they appear to have embarked upon the coastal voyage. There is no discipline amongst them and they show all the lower characteristics of animals without exhibiting any of the refinements of humans. They will foul any place in the vessel, even their own sleeping quarters, and between themselves carry out despicable practises. They seem neither to care or know right from wrong, each man should be continually supervised, an impossible task when they are so numerous and scattered throughout the vessel on deck and in holds. Pillage plunder and vandalism may be

---

[8] He was referring only to mates, as many masters and mates suffered from what we called the 'officers and engineers' syndrome, a relic from sailing ship days when mates were the only officers on board ships.

expected by any vessel embarking these gentry and little or no help from the military or police of the district can be expected.

SIGNED (E.G. Painter), 1st Mate, m.v. "DEUCALION"

In Menado, Mr Painter had said to me that "Alfie" (Alfred Holt & Co.) would be sure to give him the sack as even ship's gear had been stolen. I replied that he would be all right for a job with KPM as he had some good badjo experience! He also said that, that when he got home, he would try for a shore job as never before and, in a letter home, I said, "How I'll settle down in an office after this I don't know!!" And I didn't settle down.

As we headed south through the Macassar Strait, Kerr handed me a telegram for transmission to the Agent at Macassar. As it was already dark, static had descended on the ether so that this was impossible with only a medium-wave transmitter. When I explained to him why the message could not be sent until daylight the next day, he replied that the bloody thing was useless and that I should throw it over the side. But, as he was implying that the fault was mine, I made a mental note of the remark and incorporated it into my wireless report at the end of the voyage.

We re-crossed the equator and tied up to the oil jetty at Balik Papan in Kalimantan (Borneo) at 11am on Friday, 25 May. The badjos could hardly wait to get ashore and some of them, wearing new sarongs, coloured shirts and black hats, bought in Menado, looked quite respectable. They had done well from the sale of karung kosung/empty bags, but it was still not over as they openly carried bags ashore with them. And nothing could be done about it as they recognised no discipline at all when we were alongside. Bunkering went on throughout the night and with our fuel tanks replenished, we sailed at 6.30am on Saturday.

We docked in Macassar at 9.18am the next day and what a relief it was to get rid of the badjos after twenty-six days of their company. And a Dutchman and his wife, who were embarking as passengers to Amsterdam, were so anxious to get out of the place that they were already on the quay as we tied up. The motorboats, surfboats, and other equipment, were discharged and when the Agent came on board, it was an anxious Captain Kerr who informed him that thousands of bags had been stolen. He was in no way concerned. "That's all right Captain," he replied, "it's all covered by insurance." What a let down! And to think that someone might have lost his life trying to prevent the theft which, after all, was of no consequence. I must say, however, that I had taken a negative view all along and saw it as no part of my remit to risk my neck for gunny bags.

The old coal-burning *Gleniffer* (GRPV) was in port and when, after lunch the next day, Denis announced that he was going to pay her a visit, I said, "Bring across a crew list so that we can see who's aboard her." "OK," he replied, "but let's have one of ours to show them". I gave him one and he went off on his own. About half and hour later, I was in my cabin with some of my pals when Denis appeared at the door and I got the surprise of my life to see who was standing beside him - Joe Begg, the son of friends of my parents in Dundee. I hadn't seen Joe since the early years of the war when he had worked in an office and attended evening classes at Logie Junior Secondary School. And as our house was beside Logie, he sometimes called in before classes started. He had joined the Royal Navy and had been on board the corvette HMS *Erica* when she was sunk off Benghazi, by a mine, on 9 February, 1943. And although a gentle chap, he had completed his naval service in the Royal Marine Commandos. I already knew that he had trained as a nurse after being demobbed, but had no idea that he was serving in that capacity with Blue Funnel. But he knew I was with them and had seen my name of the crew list I had given to Denis. It was a most surprising reunion and Denis looked as pleased as Punch at having brought it about.

Joe stayed for about a couple of hours and gave me all the news about himself and his family. He was going with a nurse at Stracathro Hospital in Angus and had heard about Blue Funnel recruiting nurses from a chap who had worked beside him and who had been engaged by them. This was his first trip, but although he preferred hospital work, he intended doing a couple more in order to see places. He left at 3.30pm and we sailed at 4.38pm for Tjirebon in Java. As we moved across the harbour, Joe was with a group of his shipmates on a small island which they had reached by ship's motorboat. He was up to his waist in the water waving 'goodbye' and that was the last I ever saw of him.

The 1913-built *Lycaon* was renamed *Gleniffer* and transferred to Glen Line just prior to her current voyage which began on 6 March. She had been to Singapore and Hong Kong and had called at Labuan, British North Borneo, on her way to Macassar. As Macassar was expected to be her only Indonesian port, she was escaping the badjo ordeal and was due home at the end of July.

When we had seen the *Dolius* (GCXD) entering Melbourne as we left, I assumed that she would be homeward bound from there. I therefore thought, when we heard her on the air in the Java Sea, that she was on a fresh voyage. I was wrong: she had not been home, had come up Australia's West Coast and was bound for Djakarta. And, after Djakarta, it was back to Australia before returning to Indonesia. I learned this when I spoke to her 2nd Sparks who, I discovered, was Alan Baker who had made his first trip with me on the *Patroclus*. As that had been only a short coasting trip during September/October, 1950 and the *Dolius* had left home on 6 November, this was his first foreign voyage.

We anchored off Tjirebon at 8.36am on Wednesday, 30 May, departed at 4.54pm and anchored at Tegal at 8.12pm. In both ports we loaded bags of gaplek meel/[9]manioc meal. Work continued throughout the night in Tegal, we sailed at 8.30am on Thursday and anchored off Semarang at 3.30pm the same day.

The cargo to be loaded consisted of bagged manioc meal, bales of rubber, hides, [10]djati logs, ground tapioca roots, bags of coffee, and bales of tobacco. And as it was covered by May Bills of Lading and, as this was 31 May, the first sling had to be on board before midnight. We were a long way from the shore so that the cargo was brought out in lighters and loading began from them right away. Work continue throughout the weekend, but stopped every day at 5pm. Night work was permitted in very few Indonesian ports where a curfew usually existed. It was therefore a relief to have a quiet ship while we slept. As Darrell and I leaned over the rail watching the noisy coolies arriving, I said to him, "Decent of Calverley to give me an Australian trip."! The only thing discharged was 1290 empty copra bags carried from Menado.

The day after our arrival, I asked the Dutch Agent if he could get Bali Heads for me as there was no opportunity to go ashore. He said he would get his wife to shop for them and I gave him an adequate amount of roepiahs. And I am very grateful to the lady as, when the Agent came out to the ship, just before she sailed on 8 June, he brought the most beautiful

---

[9] Another name for the cassava plant, from the tuberous root of which tapioca is obtained.

[10] djati = real or pure. kayu djati = teak.

pair of Heads which I gave to my father. They are the carved busts of a man and a woman; the man wears a turban with a flower in it and the woman has a high-latticed headdress. They cost Rs.140 (£6.12/-/£6.60p) and I inherited them when my parents died. One of the middies got someone other than the Agent to get Bali Heads for him, but, although he had paid enough to get a good pair, those he received were small and unvarnished and carved out of a light wood instead of teak or mahogany. He was most disappointed when he saw them against mine and we were all sorry about this.

We had received mail on our return to Macassar and more greeted our arrival in Semarang. The ship was alive with copra bugs and cockroaches and the latter invaded my cabin from the bake house along the alleyway. The postscript to the letter I sent from Semarang was "Just exterminated my 624th copra bug."

We had expected to pass through the Sunda Strait, between Java and Sumatra, on the way home from Djakarta. And, as few of us had ever made the passage and seen Krakatoa, the 2nd Mate had been consulting the Admiralty Pilot/Sailing Directions for information about the volcano which, in 1883, had experienced the greatest eruption in recorded history. We were, therefore, disappointed when the Agent informed us that, after Djakarta, we were to go to Singapore for water and to pay off some of our Chinese crew.

Just before we left Semarang, an Indonesian gentleman, who had little English, asked if I would take a small packet which would be collected at Djakarta. As this was most irregular and I had no idea what it contained, I was doubtful about taking it, but he persuaded me to do so. The package was duly collected, but, in retrospect, I consider I behaved most unwisely.

With another two Dutch families on board, we sailed at 3.06pm on Friday, 8 June and docked in Tanjong Priok, Djakarta's port area, at 12.42pm the next day.

I was surprised to find that I had already met the Assistant Wharf Manager in the Liverpool Office when he was a 1st RO/Purser with Holts. His name was Joe Florio and we had a long talk. He said that, as he had his wife with him, the life was bearable. They had a nice house in Djakarta and ran a car. But, while he liked the job itself, he wasn't keen on spending a further three years in Indonesia. Joe spoke both Dutch and Malay and we had met the previous year when Holts were sending me back to the

Glengarry as No.1, after allowing me to do two voyages on her as No.2.

A further 1790 bags of manioc meal were taken on board and this, together with 218 bags of tapioca flour, meant that the *Deucalion* was fully loaded and ready for home.

We sailed for Singapore at 12.42pm on Saturday, 9 June, 1951 and it was with a sigh of relief that we bade farewell to Indonesia.

Postscript: The Dutch ruled much of the Archipelago from the early part of the 17th Century and, by 1798, the remainder of the country was under their control. And, rich in agricultural produce and minerals, the Dutch or Netherlands East Indies brought great wealth to the ruling nation. They tried unsuccessfully to regain it after the Second World War occupation by the Japanese and, on 27 December, 1949, relinquished their sovereignty, apart from that over Western New Guinea which was ceded to the independent nation of Indonesia in 1962. The Portuguese, who centuries before had fought both Dutch and English for the Islands, still held East Timor, but, in 1976, this was taken by force and incorporated into the Republic of Indonesia. Since its independence, the country has suffered considerable bloodshed under repressive governments and, even today, there is unrest due to the lack of democracy. And, right from the departure of the Dutch, the South Moluccas, which incorporates the largely Christian Island of Amboyna, have strived to become the independent Republik Maluku Selatan. At Bitung, I had received a booklet called "Facts About Holland" from Clare Mol, a friend who lived in Spijkenisse. In the section on Indonesia it says: "Holland has every reason to thank the Indies for sharing their natural wealth, whilst the Indonesian people have cause for gratitude in the higher standard of living, education, sanitation, religion and general protection." I saw no evidence of the latter claim; the women of Tanjong Priok still did their washing in the stream and, most certainly, the Indonesian people felt no gratitude.

When a ship sails in sunshine and calmer seas after being thrown about for days in heavy weather, sailors whistle tunes and there is a general feeling of cheerfulness on board. It was like this on the *Deucalion*. The seas had been calm enough and the sun had shone almost continuously, but the relief of escaping from anarchic Indonesia and heading for home was evident.   When I was in Kerr's cabin that night, he was talkative and sarcastically jovial.   On the occasion when he had railed at me for going swimming, he had said that he didn't believe I was leaving the sea, but now he asked what I intended doing when I left. "You should go in for the Ministry," he said. And when I pretended not to understand him and asked, "The Ministry of what?", he said, "The Ministry, you'd make a good parson." "I may look the part," I replied, but I'm afraid I wouldn't be very genuine." "Few of them are," said Kerr, "but it's a good steady job!"

It is 535 miles from Djakarta to Singapore and we crossed the Equator for the third time in just over five weeks.   During the passage I made up the wage accounts of the nineteen Chinese who were to be paid off and, having ascertained the amount of cash each crew member wanted to draw, I informed Kerr that I required a total of *5100 Straits Dollars. But, when he handed me the telegram addressed to Mansfield & Co., Ltd., our Agents, he requested only $780. *$1 Straits = 2/4d (11½p) and $8.50 Straits = £1 sterling.

We anchored in Keppel Harbour at 3.18pm on Wednesday, 13 June; quite close to the homeward bound *Glengarry*. The Agent came out by launch and, when I was summonsed to Kerr's cabin, I learned that he had wisely ignored Kerr's request and brought $2500 with him. When I told him what I really needed, he said that he couldn't get me any more as the banks had closed.   Kerr took $100 for himself and handed me the $2400 saying, "That's all they can get. If they're not satisfied, they can do without." And so I was left to do the dirty work of distributing less than half the amount the men had requested.

I made the payout as fairly as possible.   As the officers' draw was comparatively small, I gave them all they had asked for. To two Chinamen, who lived in Singapore and wanted $300 and $350, I gave $150 each. But the main problem was dealing with the rest of the crew. They had asked for from $50 to $100 each and were anything but pleased when they were told they could have only $20 or $30. It was not an easy job to explain the situation to fifty-five disappointed or irate Chinaman in Pidgin English.

And although I tried to convey that it was not my fault, I suspected that the less bright among them would think that it was. At any rate, there was plenty of moaning and the engine room staff complained to the Chief Engineer. And why Kerr acted as he did if beyond me. There was just no point to it and no other master ever ignored the figure I gave him. In my letter home I said, "Kerr is nothing but an ill-mannered, egotistical, selfish brute of a man. I wouldn't cross the dock with him again." We received mail on arrival and I was pleased to learn that my folks had been receiving my letters from Indonesia. Helen, on the other hand, had not heard from me for four weeks and correspondents of the other lads were having the same experience.

I personally drew $25 and, when I learned that George and Denis were going ashore that evening, I gave the money to George and asked him to get me two sharkskin shirts. They returned after midnight. George had been unable to get the shirts and Denis complained about being trailed round the shops looking for them.

The nineteen Chinamen signed off on board the next morning. Their replacements signed on and two British male passengers joined. The ship's laundry had been sent ashore and we awaited its return before sailing at 1.42pm on Thursday, 14 June.

The Singapore Free Press of Wednesday 13 June, 1951 contained the following items.

The main front page item reported on the progress of the Korean War and an item on the back page told how a financial adviser, sent to Korea by the War Office, had been unable to recommend that British troops should get the extra living-cost allowance given to men in Hong Kong. - King George VI, who had 'been suffering from catarrhal infection of the lung for two weeks', had been advised that prolonged convalescence was essential. And, as he had been a semi-invalid most of the time since 1948, there was speculation that he might abdicate in favour of Princess Elizabeth. - Guy Burgess and Donald Maclean were missing and a correspondent of the 'paper had interviewed 44-year-old W.H. Auden, the poet, at his holiday home on the Island of Ischia, near Naples. Auden had been a friend of Burgess since their Cambridge days and, as he too had once been a Communist and had fought against Franco in the Spanish Civil War, his house was 'under discreet surveillance by Neapolitan security police'. Auden considered that both men 'were almost certainly kidnapped in France'. - Only a small item covered the Malayan Emergency, but, at 10am daily the Emergency News from Kuala Lumpur was broadcast over Singapore Radio's Blue Network. - Ceylon was refusing to observe the UN embargo on strategic materials to Communist China. Mr D.S. Senanayake, the Prime Minister, urged the 'maintenance of a free flow of rubber to consumer countries' and China had offered to pay, in Swiss francs, prices for Ceylon rubber above those London buyers were prepared to pay'. - Shipping risks insurance for the Far East had yesterday been doubled. - Mr A.E.C. Drake, the general manager of The Anglo-Iranian Oil Company, said they 'could not accept any interference in the management of the company's affairs in Persia', but Persia had asked all workers to 'consider themselves employees of the Iranian National Oil Company'. On the advice of Mr Drake, a plane-a-day airlift to fly oilmen's wives and children had been started. - The Singapore Overseas Chinese Importers and Exporters Association had once again failed to arrive at any decision in its negotiations with the K.P.M. (Koninklijke Paketvaart Maatschappij) authorities to secure evidence in connection with the alleged pilferage of goods consigned to Indonesian ports by Chinese traders in Singapore. - There had been a New York State hearing concerning the growing dope traffic among school children. - South Africa had secured a 71-run victory in the first Test against England the previous day and Sydney Barnes, the 78-year-old veteran bowler, criticized Test batsman for being too defensive.

On previous voyages from the Far East, my ships had called at Port Swettenham (Kelang), Penang and Colombo.   But the already laden *Deucalion* was heading straight for Aden and I had ample time to have the cargo books and plans ready for airmail despatch from there.   It was the period of the southwest monsoon and, as soon as we rounded Sumatra, the calm seas and light airs were left behind.   Sunbathing on the deck above the wireless room, I could see and feel the line of demarcation between the Malacca Strait and the Indian Ocean.   But, with the weather still hot, I preferred to work in my cabin rather than in my inboard and airless office.

The total weight of cargo on board was 9218½ tons, but as this consisted mainly of copra (mostly consigned to the same destination), and rubber, the making of the indian ink copy of the plan was relatively easy.   In a box in the top left hand corner of the plan, I entered our ports of discharge, the total tonnage consigned to each port and its distribution.   At the top right, I entered the following in the spaces provided:

SAILED FROM (First Loading Port) Port Alma, Qld. on 10th April, 1951.
SAILED FROM (Last Loading Port) Djakarta on 11th June, 1951.

DRAFT LEAVING LAST LOADING PORT - FORWD 27'05" AFT 28'05"
FUEL OIL 1122 TONS.
FOR Amsterdam and Liverpool.

8533 tons were consigned to Liverpool, 45 tons to Amsterdam, 2 tons to Hamburg, 205 tons to Copenhagen, and ½ ton to Glasgow.   And there were options: Amsterdam/Rotterdam - 355 tons; Holland/Hamburg - 47 tons; Holland/Hamburg/Antwerp - 10 tons; Amsterdam/Rotterdam/Liverpool - 21 tons.

On the normal homeward run from the Far East, with a multitude of consignments, the making of the cargo books was an onerous task, but, as with the cargo plan, the cargo books too involved less work.

We again had a full complement of twelve passengers, ten of whom were Dutch and going to Amsterdam.   Mr and Mrs P.M. van Beek had joined at Macassar, Mr and Mrs A.P. Goossens and their 12-year-old daughter and Mr and Mrs E.F von Hombracht and their three daughters aged 5, 12 and 14 had joined at Semarang.   Mr R. Watt and Mr T.J. Denning joined at

Singapore.

All the passengers were pleasant and sociable, with the exception of Mrs Goossens. She was not long on board before she complained to Joe that the towels were being changed only once a week and, when he explained that nearly all the linen was dirty and for the wash at Singapore, she said, "It just means that my husband will have to wash them!" During the crossing of the Indian Ocean, she suffered badly from seasickness and, while we were at our meals, would wander through the saloon in her dressing gown on her way to the bathroom.

The passengers generally bore up well during the crossing although most were troubled with seasickness at times. But some people never seem to become accustomed to the motion of a ship and Mr Hombracht, who was continually asking Joe about the weather and took anti-sickness tablets every day, complained that his stomach was churning over all the time.

As we were now on the Blue Funnel mainline route, we were in radio contact with other 'Blueys'. The outward bound *Denbighshire* (GQGW) flashed past at 17 knots and her No.1 sent me his salaams. And, when we spoke to the *Calchas* (GMSS), I learned that J Finbar (Barry) O'Keefe, my No.2 on the *Medon*, was on board and going out to join the *Orestes* for a spell on the Singapore/Australia service. He asked how my studying was getting on - a rather sore point with me!

Apart from the Bosun and Carpenter, the deck crew of the *Calchas* consisted entirely of midshipmen. The senior held the rank of Leading Seaman and ten others, who had Efficient Deck Hand Certificates, were EDHs. The remaining uncertificated seven were Ordinary Seamen and Deck Boys. In addition, four midshipmen, and listed on the Articles as such, were carried.

As the mates had to log the Holt ships they sighted, we always informed them of those we heard 'on the air'. They were therefore keeping a lookout for the *Calchas* and standing on the boat deck with Darrell, I saw her just visible on our port horizon and pointed her out to him. An hour or two later, Tom Nelson rang the wireless room from the bridge to ask Darrell where the *Calchas* was now. "She's passed us," he replied, "Ian pointed her out to me." At first Tom thought that Darrell was having him on, but, when he was convinced that Darrell was not joking, he said, "Heavens, find out if they saw us and if so get the time we were abeam of each other." Darrell duly found out. They had seen us and Tom was able to cook his log and probably escape a few awkward questions at the Office as, if one ship sees another and the other doesn't see her, what sort of a watch is the bridge officer keeping? At dinner that evening, Tom said to me, "You don't want to have any of that salad - there's carrots in it and your eyesight is good enough already." "Have we passed the *Calchas* yet, sir?" asked a middy. "Just you get on with your chow," replied Tom.

In theory, and usually in practice, the worse part of the passage during the southwest monsoon is between the islands of Minicoy, in the Laccadives, and Sokotra, but this was not our experience. From Sumatra to Ceylon (Sri Lanka), there were frequent rainsqualls, but after that the sun shone almost continuously. The sea was against us, however, but, with our speed varying between 9½ and 10½ knots, this was pretty good for the old *Duke* in the monsoon. The sea remained moderate with a moderate southwesterly swell until Monday, 25 June when we were southeast of Sokotra. The wind strengthened that day and, although the sun still shone, a strong wind blew spray over the boat deck and bridge. Hoping that I would keep his last watch of the day, Darrell dropped a rather blunt hint. But, when I said, "OK", he said apologetically, "No, it's all right", expecting me to press the point. He got a shaker when I didn't, but I made it up to him by keeping a couple of his watches in the Red Sea.

Monday night proved to be the wildest night of the crossing and it blew hard until about 1pm on Tuesday when we were north of Sokotra and in its lee. Then, as we left the shelter of the Island at about 7pm, the wind and sea rose again and these conditions prevailed until about 4.30am on Wednesday, when we were entering the Gulf of Aden and abeam of Cape Guardafui. Wednesday was hot, but pleasant and, as I had the cargo plans and books ready for posting at Aden, I climbed on top of the wireless room again to acquire the tan essential to the man returning from the sea! I also felt that these spells of sunbathing renewed the energy which the hot weather sapped away. Afterwards, I washed a couple of shirts in a bucket on the boat deck before having a shower and darning a big hole in one of my white stockings. And, as I darned, Gloria (Hombracht), the 5-year-old, sat at my desk using my rubber stamps and drawing with the crayons used to colour the cargo plans. Gloria was a lovely little girl with long jet black hair and, whilst this was her first visit to my cabin, she had introduced herself to me on the first night out from Djakarta by holding up her dolly for my inspection. Perhaps because of the fuss the lads made of her, Gloria was inclined to be cheeky and, with her knowledge of the Indies, called me 'Papua' as I had had a Chinese steward almost scalp me on the way to Singapore. The steward had become most concerned when I kept telling him to take more off until I was left with a mere stubble. But it gave the lads a good laugh until they got used to it and I didn't need another haircut for months. Incidentally, Mrs Hombracht had her three daughters, none of whom spoke English, doing lessons in the saloon every morning.

We anchored off Aden's Steamer Point at 5pm on Thursday, 28 June and, as we already had sufficient fuel oil to see us to Amsterdam, left again at 10pm. There was no opportunity to buy the camera that Eric wanted me to get for him and which I might have got on the outward visit if I hadn't had trouble with the receiver.

Helen and I had been hoping that she would get leave so that we could have a holiday together, but this now seemed doubtful as a letter from her dated 4 June told me that she was leaving London that evening and was to be in the office of the recently formed European Purchasing Commission in Cologne for at least a month.

We passed through Hell's Gates at 7am the next morning. The Red Sea was approaching its hottest time and the heat did nothing to improve the poor relations which had existed between the 1st and 3rd Mates and me since Ternate. In most cases, we were all pretty well fed up with each other, but I still got on well with my immediate pals. It was hot for everyone, but worse for those in the engine room. The small electric fans, which moved in an arc of about 90°, whirred continuously in our cabins and I spent two or three nights sleeping on a stretcher on deck. But it wasn't as hot as it might have been as a northerly wind blew throughout the passage to Suez.

The tuning cord in my small Philips radio had broken and Harry and I spent Monday evening trying to fix it. It was a tricky job tying it tight. We thought we had it, but, when we were tuning in stations, it slipped and we gave up. But we were successful the following evening and it was grand to have the radio working again with numerous stations booming in on short-wave. Harry had been on the 12 to 4 watch for some time, but when he was put on from 10pm till 4am during Tuesday night, he didn't have a sleep beforehand as he thought this would make him feel worse at 10.

The deck tennis had started again and we played during the two hours before dinner as before. But, after Monday, the game was over for me as I came down heavily on a metal ring in the deck and severely sprained my left ankle. It seemed to repair quickly, but I was left with a weak ankle for many years.

We anchored in Suez Bay at 3.18pm on Tuesday, 3 July. The Agent came out to the ship, but brought no mail and, with a pilot on board, we left again at 9.12pm to join the night convoy through the Canal. I stood on deck to see Port Tewfik and thought of how I had walked its streets on previous voyages and, from the Canal bank, watched the ships entering and leaving the waterway. Few Blue Funnel men had been ashore there and even fewer had crossed the desert to Cairo, as I had done in March, 1945. I wondered if this would be the last time that I would traverse the Canal, but speculated that if Calverley were to offer me a trip to Australia, on the *Helenus* or *Ixion*, I might take it.

We exited the Canal and anchored in Port Said harbour at 11am on Wednesday. When the Agent brought out mail to the ship, I received a letter from Helen saying that, as she was returning to London on 3 July, the chance of a holiday together looked promising. In the letter I posted to my parents, I said that I felt a bit worn out with all the heat and that I looked forward to the cooler weather and to Amsterdam. I told them to write to the ship c/o Nederlandsche Stoomvaart Maatschappij Oceaan NV, Prins Hendrikkade 159, Amsterdam, C. As we had only 117 bags of coffee, for transhipment to Genoa, to discharge and nothing to load, we sailed at 3pm the same day.

We passed Cape Bon during the afternoon of Sunday, 8 July and were nearing Gibraltar on the evening of the 10th, when a group gathered round my radio to listen to the fight, at Earls Court, between Randolph Turpin and 'Sugar' Ray Robinson for the middleweight championship of the world. It was an exciting contest and Harry was on his feet shouting, "Come on, Randy." The judges awarded even points for the first two rounds and for another later on, but as Turpin won seven of the fifteen rounds, he emerged the winner and the first British boxer to win the title since it had been held by Robert Fitzimmons.

We had started playing pontoon in the smoke-room, but this was spoiled by an unpleasant incident. Our 2nd Engineer was standing behind me and refused to take his foot from my chair when I asked him to. As I could do nothing but start a brawl, I put down my cards and went to my cabin. Harry came with me. "You did the right thing," he said, "but I would have smashed his face." And I believe he would have! On an occasion when I took out my Bali Heads to look at them, Denis remarked, "When it's a cold winter's night at home, your mother will say, "Put another Bali Head on the fire, Ian!"

At 9am on Sunday, 15 July, we sent our TR to Landsendradio (GLD): GLD de GDQW Deucalion bnd Amsterdam QRB (the approximate distance between our stations is) 109 (nautical miles) SW. At about noon on Monday, 16 July, the White Cliffs of Dover were seen to port and, the following morning, we entered the North Sea Canal at Ijmuiden and passed through it to Amsterdam.

Our Dutch passengers disembarked and Tom Nelson's wife, Margaret, signed on as Supernumerary Stewardess for the trip round to Bromborough on the Mersey. After I had paid out the draw to the crew, I went into town with Harry in the afternoon and we didn't return to the ship till about midnight. The next morning, Kerr called me to his cabin and he was again in a rage. "What right had you to go ashore yesterday when there was work to be done?" he stormed. This was apparently the last straw and he was going to report me for dereliction of duty. As I had done all that was required of me, this was again complete nonsense, but there was no reasoning with the man; he just wouldn't listen to anything I said. To emphasize his authority, he told me tie up a parcel for him and, although I suspected that it was a private parcel and therefore no part of my work, I did it. From then on, the storm which awaited me at the Liverpool Office, hung over my head; although I was leaving the sea, I didn't want to resign from the Company with a black mark against my name. Yet, in spite of our relationship, Kerr had me witness his last will and testament, when crossing the Indian Ocean homeward bound, although there were many others he could have chosen.

We sailed on Wednesday, 18 July, headed back along the English Channel, and proceeded north to the Mersey. During the passage I made up the wages book of the European crew. A clerk would collect it on arrival and the official wage accounts issued by the Office. I also ascertained how much each man wanted in Channel Money as this was necessary to pay Customs Duty and other immediate incidentals. And, while bringing my dhobi up-to-date, I scorched my grey flannel trousers when pressing them.

On the morning of Saturday, 21 July, we arrived at the Pilot Station, off Point Lynas on the northwest coast of Anglesey, and a pilot boarded to take us up the Mersey. And when we moved slowly past Liverpool, someone took a picture of Joe Birch, 'Taffy' Gardiner and me with the Liver Buildings, in the background. Just prior to tying up at Lever Brothers' Dock, at that time the only privately owned dock on the Mersey, Darrell sent our final TR to [11] Seaforthradio (GLV) "Deucalion QTP (entering) Bromborough CL (closing down)". The glorious sound of 'Finished with engines' was rung on the bridge telegraph to the engine

---

[11] Seaforthradio closed on 14 May, 1960 and the station, retaining the same call sign, was transferred to Angleseyradio which itself closed on 20 December, 1986.

room, and Voyage 64 of the *Deucalion* was over.

All the copra, together with its faithful legions of copra bugs, was to be discharged directly into Lever Brothers' factory and I never look at a bar of soap without thinking of Indonesia and particularly of Ternate!

The Customs Officers boarded almost immediately and my pink Customs slip read
:

PORT OF Liverpool, 21.7.51.
SHIP (or AIRCRAFT) Deucalion @ Singapore

ARTICLES FOR DUTY and/or PURCHASE TAX	Value	Duty and Purchase Tax
Four Pairs Art Hose. Per. Pr.	£1 4s 0d	8s 0d
Twelve Plain Wood Arts	£1 0s 0d	10s 0d
	TOTAL	18s 0d
		(90p)

The Customs Officer was as lenient as usual as he lumped together all the wooden articles I had bought in Australia and the Bali Heads so that I was let off lightly.

We signed off on board the same day and, as only the Europeans were leaving the ship, this didn't take long. I paid off with £81.18s.3d and, together with my six allotments of £12, this meant that I had saved £153 during the voyage. I took only what I thought I required in cash and a Money Order for the balance. It was many years later before I possessed a bank account and credit cards had not yet been invented. Among others who boarded that day were Mr and Mrs Leigh whom we had carried to Melbourne and who had struck up a friendship with George, the Electrician. They had apparently passed us in the Red Sea on an Italian liner and I have no idea if they ever returned to settle in Australia.

Harry and I crossed the Mersey by the Woodside Ferry and went by bus to New Brighton where we spent the evening. Sunday was spent packing and I had Peter Pratt, the relieving 3rd Mate, who had been a middy on the *Samnesse* with me, take a picture of Harry and me together on the boat deck. I corresponded with Harry for two or three years. He did only one more deep-sea voyage, as 4th on the *Automedon* (GNSM), and, in September 1952, became engineer-in-charge of a Kuwait Oil Company pumping station at Ahmadi where he was joined by his wife and small son. On Monday morning, I took a taxi across to Liverpool and deposited my gear at the Left Luggage Office in Lime Street Station before reporting at India Buildings. It had crossed my mind and I hoped that Kerr might have been only bluffing when he had said he was to report me, but this notion was quickly dispelled by Calverley's questions when I confronted him at the long public desk. "How did you get on with Captain Kerr? Wasn't there some trouble between you and him in Glasgow?" Calverley always appeared nervous when one of his bosses was around and when I saw a look akin to fear come into his eyes, I realized that someone of importance with standing behind me. I turned round to find Lawrence Holt who apparently knew who I was and began talking to me. I cannot recall his exact words but the following are pretty accurate. "Was it bad in Indonesia? Were you frightened? And when you got to Amsterdam, you were tempted to get away and enjoy yourself?" As I knew that he would not listen to my side of the argument and was, in any case, talking to me like a Dutch uncle, I remained silent. He went on to say that young men didn't have any worries and finally to get off home and have a good leave. I very much doubt if Lawrence knew that I had reported Kerr's rudeness to me in Glasgow before the deep-sea voyage began, but I was very glad that I had done so.

Although I had seen Lawrence Holt during previous visits to the Office, this was the only time I met him. He was then 69 and, as Senior Partner, was head of the Company founded by his Uncle Alfred in 1865. He retired in 1953 and I believe that, as his heart was in shipping and had he still been at the helm, he would have opposed the diversification into other lines of business brought about under the chairmanship of J. Lindsay Alexander in the 1970s. It is my opinion that this diversification, for which Lindsay Alexander was knighted, led to the demise of the Blue Funnel Line. Trading under the name of "Ocean", the Company, with its headquarters now in London, still exists, but it is no longer a shipping line and all former Blue Funnel men find this sad and almost unbelievable. I quote from 'The Blue Funnel Legend' by Malcolm Falkus, published in 1990: ' "Remember Britannia, and look after my flock" is how on his retirement, Lawrence Holt bid farewell to Lindsay Alexander.'

Regarding Chinese crews, Holts employed them for over a hundred years until they were replaced by Africans. The last ship to have a Chinese crew was the *Menestheus* and when she arrived in Singapore on 1 February, 1980, the Chinese left the ship and Sierra Leoneans took their place. And as economy was always a prime consideration, I presume that West Africans had become cheaper to employ than the faithful Chinese.

My parents and Eric were in Eastbourne and I had written to say that I would join them there. But I had 'phoned Helen from New Brighton and asked her to meet me off the 5.30pm train from Liverpool. 1951 was the year of the Festival of Britain and I travelled to London on the Festival Train "Red Rose". Since the nationalization of the railways, the newly formed British Railways had been renewing the stock, clapped out by wartime use - the new trains were of such a high standard that, the first time I had boarded one, I got off again to confirm that I was in [12]3rd and not 1st Class! We spent the evening together and I stayed the night at the Endsleigh Hotel, near Euston Station. Helen had arranged to have the next day off work. We spent it at the Festival and, wanting to have more time with her, I sent the following telegram to my folks from Kings Cross Station and spent another night at the Endsleigh. "MALCOLM SOUTHVIEW PRIVATE HOTEL 38 ROYAL PARADE EASTBOURNE = DELAYED LONDON ARRIVE EASTBOURNE 11.9 WEDNESDAY = IAN". When my folks met me at the station, the first thing they asked was why I was wearing my navy blue trench coat on such a sunny day. The reason was simple. It was to cover the mark and hole I had made in my trousers when pressing them!

My father had come to Eastbourne to attend a conference but, as it lasted only a few days, Mother and Eric had joined him for a fortnight's holiday. The Southview was a small temperance hotel on the sea front. A group of mill workers from Glossop in Lancashire was there during the first week and although I preferred the second week, because it was less noisy, a young radio engineer who had been with them but had stayed on, said, "I'twere better last week"! Everyone was friendly and out for a good time so that we mixed well and when pictures were taken of the guests on the steps of the hotel, the group of five Welsh girls with whom we went boating and played tennis, were in the front row. We enjoyed an evening at the Pierrots and I remember a sketch involving a couple and their 'son' at the tea-table. When the son said, "Pass the butta please, Dad", the father objected to his pronunciation of the word 'butter'. The son repeated the request pronouncing the word correctly and the father said, "That's betta." Among the amusements on the pier was the artist REX who did cutout silhouettes of clients in a matter of minutes. I still have the excellent one he did of me.

---

[12] There was no 2nd Class until June, 1956.

We climbed to the top of Beachy Head, went to Battle, where we were in the old mint house, and to Canterbury. And, of course, my folks wanted to see the Festival of Britain. As this was an opportunity to see Helen again, I went up to London with them on Thursday, 2 August and my picture was taken beside the 'SEA AND SHIPS' sign in front of the exhibit which housed a stand showing the work of the GPO Coast Stations. I left to meet Helen when she finished work at the Millbank office at 5pm and, as we strolled in Regents Park, I gave her one of the brooches I had bought in Menado and a headscarf. We had supper in Lyons Quebec Café at Marble Arch before I saw her home.

Helen lived in the hostel for young ladies - The Hall, at 6A Primrose Hill Road in Hampstead. I left her at 11.15pm, took the tube into town from Chalk Farm Station and caught the last train to Eastbourne from Victoria. It was after two in the morning before I got back to the hotel and at breakfast the jocular chef called me a 'dirty stop-out'! Incidentally, Millbank House, in which the Board of Trade headquarters were situated, was owned by Shell and Douglas Bader, the legless wartime pilot, worked in the building.

We left Eastbourne on the morning of Saturday, 4 August. I travelled up to London Victoria with my folks, but left them there as they were flying to Glasgow. I had only my leather grip with me as I had deposited my sea-going gear at the Left Luggage Office at Kings Cross. And after wandering around London and whiling away the time by going to the pictures, I boarded the overnight train to Dundee on which I had booked a sleeper. When I arrived in Dundee the next morning, I was surprised to find a family friend meeting me with the news that my folks were not yet home. Their 'plane had been delayed in leaving London due to a strike so that it had arrived in Glasgow too late for them to catch the last train to Dundee. They had spent the night in Glasgow and would be returning later in the day. They had wired our friend to meet me as I had no key to the house.

I waited until mid August before going down to the telephone box near our house to tell Calverley that I was leaving the sea. His reply surprised me. "I know you don't like being purser," he said, "so you can have the [13]*Kimanis*. There would be no purser's work, you'd be the only operator and you'd take her to Singapore and return home as passenger." It was a tempting offer. The *Kimanis* was completing her fitting-out at the Caledon Shipyard in Dundee and this would have given me my only opportunity of sailing out of the Tay. But as I had had enough of the Far East and the break had to be made sometime, I stuck to my decision.

In my letter of 21 August, confirming my resignation, I requested coasting duties while seeking shore employment. Calverley's replied that, as they were fully staffed, he couldn't promise this, but would call upon me if necessary. As he also said that he would be pleased to forward a reference if one were required, I took up the offer and received the following:

ALFRED HOLT & Co.   India Buildings,

Ocean Steam Ship Company Limited   Liverpool, 2.
The China Mutual Steam Navigation Co. Ltd.

THE BLUE FUNNEL LINE.

   Telegraphic Address,
"ODYSSEY", LIVERPOOL.
TELEPHONE No. 5630 CENTRAL.   8th September, 1951.

To Whom it may Concern.

   This is to certify that Mr. I. M. Malcolm joined this Company as a Radio Officer/Purser in July, 1943, and served with us in that capacity until September, 1951, when he resigned entirely of his own accord in order to seek shore employment.

---

[13] The *Kimanis*, owned by the Straits Steamship Company in which Holts had an interest, was launched on 22 March, 1951. She was a small passenger-cargo ship of 3100 grt, for operation between Singapore and North Borneo, and could carry 40 first-class passengers, 24 second-class and a further 500 in her shelter decks. Holts provided the crew to take her to Singapore.

During the whole of this period the Masters under whom he served have reported him to be strictly sober, hard working, trustworthy and efficient.

ALFRED HOLT & CO

Holts operated their pension scheme by taking out policies on our behalf with the Liverpool & London & Globe Insurance Company (later taken over by Royal) and I was sent my policy so that I could continue or cash it. The sum assured was £813. Although the annual premium of £25.16.0 was onerous on the low salary I had to begin with, I did continue it. It had been taken out in 1950, when I was 25, and I received £3662.31p, in 1985, when I was 60.

I had always dealt with the office of the ROU (Radio Officers' Union) at 7 Collingwood Street, Newcastle and on 13 September I sent a letter of resignation and a Money Order for £2.12/- to clear my account. I had been a member since July, 1943 and my Member's No. was 16780.

Postscript: Helen and I did have a holiday together, in Aberdeen, in August, 1951. From 15 September till 28 October she was again on the Continent with her Assistant Secretary boss. This time it was to the GATT (General Agreement on Tariffs and Trade) Conference, in the Palais des Nations in Geneva, which the Japanese were allowed to attend only as observers. On 2 November I received a telegram telling me to 'phone her. The news was that the transfer to Dundee that she had requested had come through and she was to work at the District Valuer's Office.

I found it difficult to get a clerical job, but eventually landed in the Production Control Department of the National Cash Register Company at £6-10/- a week – a considerable comedown from my previous salary of £50 a month with all found. The jute trade was diminishing and the NCR, Dundee's largest employer, paid better wages although mine didn't appear to reflect this.

The main part of my job consisted of supplying the production line with the components required to build the cash registers. Towards the beginning of every week, I was told how many machines were to be built, together with their destinations, as foreign countries required different currency keys. I then worked out how many washers, springs, etc. were to be issued to the workbenches from the stores. Although this required no great mental ability, it required concentration and was extremely tedious and boring. To rub salt into the wound, a work's foreman came to see me one day and asked me to come into the workshop to have a look at the bins at the benches which contained the components. They were overflowing so that the foreman said, "You'll have to stop issuing the stuff." And, as I was meticulous in my work, this meant that the cards which I used and which contained the information as to how many of a certain part were required to build a machine, were incorrect.

The figures on the source-cards were gleaned from engineering drawings - a process known as 'a breakdown'. When I was approached by the Accounts' Department to do one such breakdown, I found that the parts were difficult to identify as the drawing wasn't clear, but was later told that it was the best they had ever had! The NCR lost their lead in the world market when better cash registers were produced in Italy, etc.

Another thing which irked me was that the weekly program was continually changed after I had been working on it for perhaps two days. When this happened, I had to scrap my work and begin the whole thing again. There was indeed one week when the programme was changed three times so that my total week's work was discarded and, on Friday, the head clerk asked me to work overtime during the weekend. "Get the bloke who keeps changing the programme to come in," was my answer. Only my evenings and weekends with Helen kept me sane.

I was never so bored and depressed in my life and what added to this was the lack of freedom. We had to clock in and out of the building and once when I was leaving the Department, the head clerk, who had been a baker, asked were I was going. When I replied, "The toilet" and he said, "There are too many out of the Department already", I ignored the injunction and went just the same.

During the two years I put up with this, I tried for other jobs and could have had one with a travel agent called Sibald if I had been prepared to move for £6-10/- a week when my wage, by then, was £7. Another job offered to me was with the Dundee, Perth and London Shipping Company. They had not advertised for a clerk, but, thinking that a job in shipping would be of much more interest, I wrote to them and Mr Cowper, the Managing Director, interviewed me one Saturday morning. The interview went well. "I like the look of you", he said. "I'm prepared to offer you a job." But when he learned that my wage at the NCR was £7, he exclaimed that was more than his chief clerk got and that was the end of that.

And so it was, after two years in purgatory, I decided that Dundee held nothing for me and, in August, 1953, applied to the GPO for a job on their coast stations.

I was called for interview to the Overseas Telecommunications Department at GPO Headquarters in St. Martin's Le Grand, London outside of which stands a statue of Rowland Hill. The main part of the interview, as far as I remember, was the inevitable Morse test. After the interview I visited the Tower of London and, in the evening, went to see South Pacific on stage at the Theatre Royal Drury Lane. The GPO subsequently offered me a post. I wanted to work on the small station at Stonehaven (GND), but was told that there was already a waiting list for that station. There were vacancies at Burnham Radio and Wick. I opted for Wick so they sent me to Burnham which was, in fact, Portishead Radio Station which I had so often communicated with when at sea.

I arrived, together with my motorbike which accompanied me on the train journey from Dundee, at Highbridge Station at 11.25 pm on the miserable foggy night of Friday, 9th October. I had to change trains at Bristol and I was the only person to alight at Highbridge. There was the depressing moan of foghorns from the Bristol Channel and a lone oil-skinned railwayman carrying an oil lamp appeared to await my arrival so that he could go home. It was reminiscent of joining an almost deserted ship on a winter's night. I drove into Burnham-on-Sea and located the digs which the Post Office had arranged for me. Another newcomer to the Radio Station had been kind enough to wait up for me and I had a cup of tea before turning in.

The accommodation to which the Post Office had directed me was run by Mrs Jenner who was known to almost everybody at the Radio Station as so many of them had been directed to her establishment. I spent the first night in her house in Cross Street before being transferred to accommodation above her café on the Esplanade where a number of new boys were boarded. The place was not very clean and my bed remained just as the previous occupant of the room had left it. There was, however, a large sitting room overlooking the Esplanade and when I sat there with all the fellows the evening after my arrival, I felt happy to be back among my own kind.

We all had to undergo a training period of about six weeks in what was known as the School. This was merely a big hut beside the main building and the two main activities were improving our Morse speed and learning to type. As I had learned to touch-type at night school before going to sea, this was like a holiday for me. The Post Office made you pass a Morse test at 27 wpm plus an interview board and language tests in both French and German before accepting you as an Established Civil Servant. Joe Wynn, a long serving Post Office operator nearing retirement, was in charge of the School. He was a pleasant man so that we enjoyed ourselves. Towards the end of the training, we were each attached to an operator on the Station and began to take part in the regular work. I landed an awkward cuss whom I didn't care for at all. This somehow was recognised and another fellow took me under his wing. He was a chap I took to. He was one of the few who hadn't been at sea, but had held a commission in the army. His name was Mulholland and, after I had left the Service, he became O/C at Portishead. During this training period, we remain on 9 to 5 day work only. Then, just as I was reconciled to working at Portishead, they transferred me to Wick! So my motorbike and I got on the train again and headed for the far north of Scotland.

I arrived in Wick on Tuesday, 8th December and was to stay almost a year at Wickradio/GKR where the duty system was ridiculous. Bruce Mackie, the O/C (Officer-in-Charge), was a slim clean-cut dedicated Post Office man in his fifties who wore half-moon glasses. His experience of the sea had been time spent on a Post Office cable ship. I seem to recall that we had to pay for the Post Office type of propelling pencil which we used, although I may be wrong in that. These pencils were used by counter clerks and had a serrated bulbous piece at the end which was designed for telephone dialling. We were certainly issued with the leads and, one day, I went to the O/C's office for a lead for the pencil. I have never been wasteful, but Mr Mackie issued one lead at a time and, on this occasion, he let the lead go before I had hold of it so that it shattered on the floor. This was a minor catastrophe!

There was no rotation of duties. The duties were fixed so that, once you were told your hours for the week, that was it until further notice. My duty was changed a number of times, but all the duties I worked gave me neither a Saturday nor a Sunday off. The duties were based on whether the number of operators available was 14, 15 or 16. An example of one of these duties was 'Duty K' based on a working complement of 16 operators:

Sunday	12 - 6 pm	
Monday	9 - 12	1 - 4.40 pm
Tuesday	8 - 2 pm	11 - midnight
Wednesday	midnight - 9 am	
Thursday	Rest Day	
Friday	5.30 pm - midnight	

Saturday   12 - 2 pm   5 - 11 pm

During my time at Wick, not only did I never have a weekend off, but sometimes I was forced to work part of my rest day when the Thorshavn cable, the link between the Faroes and Denmark, broke down. When this happened, a postman would come to my door with a telegram requesting/ordering me to report for duty. I then had the onerous task of copying all the traffic sent by Morse from Thorshavn, and this was sometimes difficult to read due to poor reception. The messages were sent on to London by teleprinter. I hated that Thorshavn cable. It was always breaking down, but, of course, there was the consolation of being paid 4/8d for the one hour you had to work and which had completely ruined your only day off! My wage was less than £10 a week for a 48-hour week. It wasn't long before I put my name down on the 'transfer lists' for Oban and Portishead.

Some operators regarded Wick as the 'last outpost of the Empire'. Helen and I were married shortly after I went to Wick and we were happy living there. We rented a nice furnished house not far from the Radio Station for £8 a month and my rest day was usually spent touring Caithness on our motorbike. It was a new world for us - flat and generally treeless, but with magnificent cliff scenery. The Radio Station was the 'fly in the ointment'. I remember someone at Portishead jokingly saying to someone in my presence "He *volunteered* for Wick!"

The work at Wickradio was almost exclusively with the trawlers sailing out of Hull, Grimsby, Fleetwood, Aberdeen and Granton (near Edinburgh) to the fishing grounds off Iceland, the Faroes, Bear Island and the White Sea. When I later worked at Portishead, I sometimes heard trawlers calling Wick on H/F (High Frequency i.e. short-wave) and they particularly wanted Wick because a reduced rate applied if they cleared traffic through any coast station other than Portishead. This, in effect, generally meant Wick as it was the only station, apart from Portishead, with H/F W/T (Short Wave Wireless Telegraphy i.e. Morse) which they needed for long distance working. We also had 2 mc/s R/T (Radio Telephony) (Amplitude Modulation/AM) which, under good conditions, could be used over fair distances, plus the normal medium wave W/T.

I had arrived in Wick in time for Christmas, 1953 and was still 'green' as I had been away from the sea for two years. I was on the 500 kcs/s (the W/T calling and distress frequency) position when a British ship (not a trawler) called up with a telegram and gave his working frequency as 410 kcs/s. I vaguely thought this an unusual frequency to choose, but said OK and took his short telegram on this frequency. The whole operation took only two or three minutes and I thought nothing more about it until some months later I received a letter from Head Office asking me to explain why I had taken a telegram on the frequency reserved for direction-finding! There was a sheaf of papers attached to the letter. Nordeich Radio/DAN had made the complaint and there was a letter of apology from the ship's R/O who tried to excuse himself by saying it was Christmastime and other frequencies were busy. No doubt I recorded some equally feeble excuse, but, after that, I didn't feel friendly disposed towards Nordeich! We were on friendly terms with Bergen/LGN who were, so to speak, just across from us as we regularly exchanged lists of call signs of ships for whom traffic was held. But, when it came to the misuse of frequencies, the trawlers were very culpable, as many of them would hold conversations with other vessels on 'ship to shore' frequencies. Many a Link Call was spoiled by this inconsiderate practice.

One of the trawler companies always made the friendly gesture of sending a large cod to the Station for Christmas. That Christmas I was there, nobody wanted it and it smelt a bit high anyway! The O/C presented it to a 'needy' family who could have lived off it for a week.

Typical of Wick, I was on duty Christmas Day and I remember a trawler skipper saying to me "Merry Christmas, Wick" when he was 'out there' in atrocious weather enjoying himself! You couldn't but respect the men who sailed in such dangerous waters and under such appalling conditions. "May Day, May Day, May Day" might be heard on R/T and nothing more.

I was also on duty on Old Year's Night and was due to travel south on the morning train to be married in Dundee. I was living in the Rosebank Hotel which was owned by Mrs Sutherland who reduced her rates to permanent guests. Knowing Scotland on Hogmanay, I asked Isobel, one of the waitresses/chambermaids, if I'd be able to get breakfast as usual when I came off duty in the morning. "Yes, that'll be all right," she assured me. "Are you sure?" I insisted. "Definitely," she said. And so I boarded the morning train not only tired but hungry. You could have stolen the Rosebank and everything in it that morning! I hoped then to get something to eat when the train reached Inverness in the afternoon, but the town was deserted and I had to settle for a bar of chocolate from perhaps the only small shop open. Even the railway station had a forlorn look about it with a porter literally staggering under his indulgences of the night. Although the Rosebank let me down on that occasion, I liked living there. It was homely, comfortable and the food was good and plentiful. Isobel was a star and a terrible flirt and I sometimes had difficulty in understanding what she was saying. One of the dishes was a dessert called 'Queen of Puddings' which she described as "Quin a Piddin'" and when I said that I didn't know what she was saying she repeated the name in exactly the same way. Mrs Sutherland had a Pekinese called 'Chinky' which Isobel referred to as Jenky.

Helen and I were married on Thursday the 7th of January, 1954. Our honeymoon consisted of two nights in Edinburgh and we travelled north by train on the Saturday as I had to be back at work the following day. The train left Waverley Station at 10 am and there was a panic to make it, as we slept in and were wakened by the maid. In these days, the train journey was painfully slow as, between Inverness and Wick, the train stopped at every station. In winter, there was one train a day and it went only as far as Helmsdale. We disembarked there and travelled the remaining 37 miles by bus; arriving in Wick at 10 pm and to the most pleasant surprise of a roaring fire in the living room of our new home.

Our home was Lorne Cottage, East Banks in the district of Pulteneytown. It is the end house of a row of terraced houses and was within easy walking distance of the Radio Station. We rented it from Mrs Nellie Anderson who no doubt arranged to have the welcoming fire prepared for us. To say that I came across the house by accident is prosaically true as the two elderly ladies who had previously occupied it were found dead due to an escape of gas. Mrs Anderson was a small thin elderly lady who kept house in Edinburgh for her doctor nephew who worked for the Scottish Office. Before my departure for Dundee, she had interviewed me and because I looked like her nephew and my name was also Ian, I was considered to be a suitable tenant.

During our tenancy, Mrs Anderson appeared only once when she arrived, unexpectedly, like a whirlwind. I was at work when she arrived at the house and 'created' because a shrub at the door hadn't been pruned. By the time I got home, however, she had calmed down. She was in her seventies and was fearful of the condition in which she would find her house. When Helen had shown her that the house was in good order, Nellie knew that she was out of order and became very nice. When we left Wick, she wrote a letter regretting our departure.

I soon came to realize that it was an objective to acquire as much traffic as possible, even if it was at the expense of another coast station (particularly

Stonehaven/GND) and when it came to handling distress, paperwork was of paramount importance. I handled only one distress and this was on my last night at Wick. There were only two of us on at night and I was on the W/T point. At 2345 a ship called GKR on 500 kcs/s in very slow stumbling Morse. I sent AS SP (Wait [14]Silence Period) to him and he came back very slowly with ._ _ _ ... .. _. _._ (am sink....) By the time he got that length I had the D/F on him and took a bearing, then asked him to send long dashes. He ignored the request and said to listen for him on R/T where my colleague picked him up. That was the beginning on a hectic night and I had the experience of activating the Auto Alarm and the whole of Europe waiting for me to send the SOS. And when it came to a distress, two operators were not enough. I would turn up the 'wick' at the W/T console and dash next door to the landline room. The first thing was to notify the coastguard by telephone and, when I got through, what sounded like an older man, replied with, 'Aye, jist a meenet till I get a pencil'! RAF, Pitreavie had to be informed, by teleprinter, as did Lloyds of London whose tugs sat with 'steam up' hoping for salvage. We got help to the ship in the shape of a Dutch destroyer and one or two other ships which stood by her. The ship did not sink. She was the Norwegian *Granfoss* and made Lerwick under tow. And, in the middle of all this we had an XXX (Urgency Signal) to contend with. As Helen and I were to leave Wick on the 8.35 am train bound for Somerset, a colleague was kind enough to relieve me at 8 am. It was with great relief that I boarded that train and I often wondered at not being questioned about the paperwork!

Wick was an extremely busy station at that time. There was a lot of W/T work and a lot of Link Calls on R/T; Wick was the link between the R/T call from the ship and the telephone in the home or office. Link Calls cost 7/6d for 3 minutes and I must, in the beginning, have had a different Duty from 'Duty K' described above because, as a new boy, I was on the R/T point at 9 am on a Saturday morning. I felt under extreme pressure at that position as, it was the time in the week when all the trawlers seemed to want to speak to their offices. My first job was to read the weather report on 2182 kcs and I knew that as soon, as I finished speaking, the air would be absolute bedlam with trawlers calling Wick! It is only with experience you stay calm in such a situation: "*Kingston Diamond*. This is Wickradio. Your turn is No.1 ....". And these private calls were only relatively

---

[14] On 500 kcs, the W/T calling and distress frequency, the Silence periods were from 15 to 18 minutes and from 45 to 48 minutes past every hour. On the Radio Telephony calling and distress frequency of 2182 kcs/s, they were from 0 to 3 minutes and from 30 to 33 minutes past every hour.

private as the citizens of Wick just had to tune across the dial of their wireless sets to hear Wickradio loud and clear. Helen used to listen in to me doing my stuff on a Saturday morning when I would give a couple of clicks of the tongue as a message to her!

I had been in Wick only a few months when I was given the opportunity to appear before a Civil Service Commission in order to become an Established civil servant. I, naturally, wanted Establishment, but the Commission was to sit in London! I thought that this was discriminatory and ridiculous. Two other operators, Scott and Murray, were also called to London and I tried to get them to agree that none of us should go, but without success. It wasn't just the length of the journey which irritated me, but the fact that we were to be given only 3rd Class rail travel, no expenses and only sufficient time off to attend the interview if we travelled day and night in both directions! We even had, initially, to pay the rail travel, but this could be claimed from the Commission. The other two went to London and became Established civil servants. I did not.

On these occasions, you have to play the game according to the rules imposed on you, so I wrote a letter to the O/C stating that I would not be attending the Commission 'because I could not afford the obvious expense involved' and awaited the call to his office. To his civil service mind, what I was doing was little short of lunacy. "Do you mean to tell me, old man, that you're not attending the Board because you can't raise the wind?" whereby I stubbornly refused to amplify what I had said in my letter. He then offered to lend me the money, but I turned down his kind offer! There was then a 'phone call from the office of the Inspector of Wireless Telegraphy in London to the O/C on the subject. Who was this idiot refusing to attend a Board? And I knew of the call because I received it at the exchange board and passed it on to the O/C.

But the punch line came a week or two after the two newly Established civil servants were back from London. We were paid weekly in cash, and on Thursday which was my Rest Day. Everyone collected their brown envelopes that day when even the men off duty went up to the station to collect. I was the exception and generally collected my pay the following day when I returned to work. But, quite unintentionally, I completely forgot to collect on that occasion and, a day or two later, the O/C came into the landline room when I was on my own. He was smiling as he handed me the envelope saying, "Your pay, old man". I couldn't help smiling too! On my last night on duty, he came over from his house on the premises late at night to wish me well.

When I had been transferred from Portisheadradio to Wickradio in December, 1953, I had received no expenses and hadn't, in fact, expected any because I had initially indicated my wish to go to Wick. Transfer expenses were generally paid and, due to my 'dispute' with the Post Office which I had brought to the notice of the Union, I raised this point. Ray Dobson, the UPW Representative at Portishead, took this up with London HQ who claimed that I had not been transferred, but had gone of my own volition. When the point was pursued, however, W. Swanson, a Wicker in a senior position in London, conceded that I had indeed been transferred and I benefited to the tune of over £30! Swanson disclosed in his letter to Dobson that he knew of Bruce Mackie's offer to lend me money to attend the Commission.

In November, 1954 my name came to the top of the transfer list for Portishead and I readily accepted the offer. A six-day week was worked at all the coast stations, but the split shifts (cf. the Saturday of Duty K above) plus the fixed duties were, perhaps, peculiar to Wickradio and certainly did not exist at Portishead. I've always been glad that I had the experience, however, of living in Caithness and of gaining insight into that world of the trawlermen which has since disappeared. In 1990, I returned to Wick for the first time in 36 years when Douglas Cameron and his wife, Lilian, invited me to stay at their holiday home at Keiss, about ten miles to the north. Like every other place, there is a considerable number of new houses, but, nevertheless, the town had changed very little. We called at the, by then, British Telecomm. Radio Station and were made very welcome by the two lads on duty, but the inside of the building had changed out of all recognition. All the consoles had gone and the operators, both ex seafarers, were housed in a smaller back room where they sat looking into computer screens.

And so I returned to Portisheadradio and remained there for two years; until I left the Post Office to train as a teacher in Edinburgh in September, 1956. I was back at the station for only a matter of weeks when my name came up on the transfer list for Oban. If I had been offered Oban while at Wick, I would have taken Oban, but shuffling up and down the length of Great Britain can get a bit tedious! I declined the offer and I'm sure I wouldn't have enjoyed the work there nearly as much as I did at Portishead. Obanradio, located at Connel to the north of Oban, was closed in 1982.

127

The transmitters of Portisheadradio were located at Portishead, in Somerset, but the radio station was at Highbridge and we lived in Highbridge's twin town, Burnham-on-Sea. It's impossible to tell when you cross from one to the other, but both towns have their shopping centres and Burnham is, perhaps, the more attractive and a holiday town on the Bristol Channel. The Radio Station, known locally as the 'Woirless' Station, was a fairly large red brick building standing in fields off a country lane just inside Highbridge territory. I used to wonder at the utter desolation of it from the outside. The place seemed deserted and no sounds came from it while, in the adjacent fields, sheep grazed under the rhombics.

In my day, anybody could wander into the place and there was a total lack of security. It wasn't even thought of. When I was shown round the place many years later, there was a security guard at a gate which formerly hadn't been there. He examined passes before raising the metal bar to allow cars to enter or leave. When I worked there, the operators had old bikes usually purchased from Syd, the handyman from the Potteries who was the recognised bike dealer. During that later visit, there was at least one locked metal door between sections of the building and the operators carried a plastic card to allow them to pass through the door. After leaving Portishead, I remained in touch with Gerry Knott, who was also ex-Blue Funnel and became the Union Rep. He asked me if I'd like to see round the place and as we entered the front door there was an operator standing there. When Gerry said to this chap, "Do you remember, Ian?", he immediately answered, "Yes, you left to go to Edinburgh University, didn't you?" After so many years, it was nice to be remembered and without a moment's hesitation.

When I worked at Portishead, the Station was laid out in the shape of a cross with the Control Area in the centre. From the main door to this area were the O/C's office, the engineers' workshop and the accounts' room. On either side of the Control Area were long wings where the operators sat at the H/F points (Morse only) working the ships. One of these wings was in permanent use while the other was brought into use when the place became really busy. There were pictures of ships on the wall in the permanently used wing and I remember one of Cunard's *Berengaria*. Directly in front of the Control Area was the landline room housing the teleprinters used for incoming and outgoing traffic, page printers connecting the station directly with the Naval Station in Whitehall, a machine connecting us directly with the weather forecasting centre (perhaps Bracknell) and a number of typewriters for the typing of Ship Letter Telegrams (SLTs). This room also contained the small medium-wave operating position which was Burnham-on-Sea Radio (GRL). And don't let anyone tell me that a state-owned enterprise cannot be efficient. Portishead was extremely efficient yet a pleasant place to work with a relaxed atmosphere.

There was a rotation of duties at Portishead, so that you had a different set of hours and a different day off each week and every so often a Saturday and Sunday off. Some years after I left the station, a vote was taken on having a five-day week, but the operators voted to continue working the six days as I think the number of hours was only slight reduced. The hours you worked were never the same two days running so that mealtimes were irregular and the one nightshift every week really was designed to throw your system out of gear. There were no 'split shifts' at Portishead. There was a great deal of 'overtime' going and, although the hours were onerous enough, some 'overtime kings', as we called them, were always looking for it. Almost every week, compulsory 'overtime' was shown against my name on the duty board and I would show that I wanted rid of it. The symbol of a flag was used in the transaction, but I can't remember whether you drew a flag to get rid of the 'overtime' or whether it indicated acceptance. The 'kings' kept their eyes on the duty board and grabbed everything going.

The only time I did overtime willingly was before I departed for Edinburgh when I knew money was going to be tight. The reason for all the overtime was a permanent shortage of staff and if they hadn't taken on operators with 2nd Class tickets, the situation would have been even worse. Of all the fellows who started with me, I was the only one with a 1st Class ticket. The 2nd Class boys could be employed at lower wages and in a temporary capacity for years. Towards the end of my time, some of them got their notice as men with 1st Class tickets became available and ironically some of them went into the Admiralty Wireless Service or GCHQ and got higher wages than we did! Attempting to investigate this, our Union, the Union of Post Office Workers (UPW), was told that the work they did was secret so that it could not be compared with ours! There was a constant turnover of men for various reasons. Some decided that they would rather be at sea where the wages were higher anyway. One guy who came to Wick decided he didn't like the look of the place and caught the train back south the following morning! Another went to a commonwealth radio station. I considered this last option myself and still have the rates for the Aussie coast stations where, the further north you went, the more money you got. You could be well off in Darwin, but even better off in Papua New Guinea!

The Area System was in operation for ships registered anywhere in the British Commonwealth or the Republic of Ireland. The world was divided into eight Areas, with some subdivision of the larger Areas although, for some unknown reason, there wasn't an Area 4. Each Area was served by a Transmitting and Receiving Station plus at least one Receiving Station. Portisheadradio was the Area Transmitting and Receiving Station for Area 1 which was subdivided into Areas 1A, 1B and 1C. Area 1A covered the Atlantic to 40°W and the Arctic Ocean to 45E. Its southern limit was 25°N and included the Mediterranean to 20°E. (Halifax, NS was the Area Station for Area 9 which was the Atlantic west of 40°W and south to 35°N.) Area 1B was the Mediterranean east of 20°E and the whole of the Red Sea. Area 1C was the Atlantic south of 25°N and east of 40°W, and south of 35°N, west of 40°W. The southern limit of Area 1C was 10°S. The Area System was primarily a defence network of fixed naval radio stations so that a ship could send its traffic to any area station for relay to its destination without any additional charge. (Once, when on the *Glengarry* in the Red Sea, I had a message for the UK and couldn't raise Portishead, so sent it to Wellington, NZ. This seems ridiculous to the layperson, but, of course, distance to the office of destination was irrelevant.)

The work at Portisheadradio was interesting and varied. Everybody took a turn at doing every job and it was organised so that you never did the same job for more than two hours.

Incoming traffic for the UK arrived at the Station in two ways: (a) by direct communication with the ship and (b) over the direct teleprinter link with the Naval Station in Whitehall where messages were received from other Area Stations over the fixed naval network. A careful check was kept of the numbers of all telegrams received from ships and in the middle of the floor in the Control Area, an operator was kept busy on this job alone. If telegram No.2 were received and there was no record of No.1, there was an immediate enquiry to the ship. If the operator at an H/F point was still in communication with the ship, it could be contacted in this way. If not, a message would be put into the Area Broadcast. Obviously it was important under this system to know where the ship was and, more importantly, to which Area Broadcasts the ship's Radio Officer was listening. This was where the TRs (messages which gave this information) came in and within the same Control Area, TRs were continually being filed for reference. It was incumbent on the ship's R/O to let us know in advance when the ship was due to enter a different Area and exactly when he would begin to listen to the traffic lists of that Area.

In the permanent H/F wing, the operators sat at desks in two rows facing opposite directions and in one of these rows were about half a dozen RN telegraphists who were there to establish a naval presence. The UPW had apparently tried to get rid of these lads without success. The telegraphists were generally in the care of a portly and jovial Petty Officer Telegraphist although a Lieut. showed up on occasion. The telegraphists worked only at these H/F points where they were given the bulk of naval traffic, but also worked merchant ships just as we did. We, conversely, took traffic from naval ships and acquired some knowledge of the gradation of naval priority signals. I took my first priority message seriously until I learned it was to arrange a football match when the ship docked at Plymouth! Everything was priority with the Royal Navy!

On the desk in front of each operator were a Marconi CR150 receiver, a block-capitals-only typewriter, a rotating selective aerial switch and a logbook. We were each supplied with heavy PO earphones, which we stored in our individual metal lockers when we went off duty, but one or two individuals had purchased their own light-weight 'phones. We worked in small teams with one man on what was called 'search-point'. Each team worked on a different frequency and varied in size according to the number of ships waiting to clear traffic on that frequency. The job of 'search-point' was to listen for ships calling. He would select an omnidirectional aerial then, when he heard a ship calling, say GKL, (a different call sign was used on every frequency, but all Portisheadradio call signs began GK), he would move the rotating aerial selection switch to select the relevant directional aerial so as to hear the ship as clearly as possible. If all the operators in his team were busy, he would 'go out' to the ship with e.g. GNCS GKL QRY1 (to GNCS from GKL your turn is No.1) and there would often be a number of ships at great distances from one another waiting to clear their traffic. When the ship called, he would indicate on which frequency he would send his telegram/s by QSS followed by the last three digits of the frequency (the first digit(s) was obvious as he was already on say 6 or 8 mc/s - not mhz in these days). When an operator finished working a ship and was ready for another he would indicate this to the 'search-point' who would give him the call sign of the ship, the frequency it would transmit on, the number of telegrams it had to send and the best aerial to select to hear it. The 'search-point' then crossed the ship off his list and adjusted the QRY number when he heard another ship calling. The operator who had been given GNCS would transmit to the ship GNCS GKL UP. The listening ship would answer GKL de GNCS R UP and move to his transmitting frequency. When he got there he would send GKL de GNCS QRK? (What is the readability of my signal?) The operator at GKL would now be listening for him on that frequency and would send GNCS GKL K (the invitation to transmit) and the R/O would send his message. We were at liberty to either type or write the messages and when, having sent the telegram, the ship was collating numbers and difficult words in the text, we timed and initialled the telegram while still listening and placed it in the conveyor-belt channel which ran between the two rows of operators to the Control Room where it dropped into a metal container. It was the job of a tall, balding and gentle uniformed postman to take the messages from that container to the man recording their receipt. Down in that day's record would go GNCS 1 and the telegram would be put into another conveyor-belt channel to carry it into the landline room for onward transmission, by teleprinter, to the town of, or nearest to, its destination.

All the operators on a particular frequency used the same transmitter and when the transmitter was in use a red light located in a small box on each desk indicated this by blinking in unison with the Morse being sent. When you wanted to 'speak' to the ship, your hand was poised on the Morse key as you watched for the blinking to stop. When this happened, you 'dived in' and if two of us 'dived in' together, the ships' R/Os would hear a momentary slurring of GKL's gruff note until one of us gave way.

The hardest work I did at Portishead was when we operated a 'work to rule' for more money. When we were operating normally, we didn't operate according to the rule book i.e. Ship's call sign 3 times de GKL 3 times, etc. It was just as I've stated above; GNCS GKL sent only once with even the 'de' omitted. The big passenger liners were on the seas in these days and ships such as the *Lizzie* (GBSS) and the *Mary* (GBTT) had scores of telegrams to send and no time to waste. During the 'work to rule', it was GBSS 3 times de GKL 3 times, etc. and I could sense the amazement/disbelief of the guy at the other end when I worked my first passenger ship under these conditions. I could picture his face and what he said to a colleague in the radio room about this 'new boy/twit' at Portishead until it dawned on them all that they were dealing with a reformed Portishead. Complaints began to pour in from the shipping companies - just imagine the *Queen Mary* showing up at Southampton without Cunard knowing exactly when she would berth - no pilot in readiness, no trains to convey passengers up to London, no etc. etc! And it was the same with the outgoing traffic. The gummed strips of telegrams were spewing in from teleprinters and coiling up in the tall elliptical metal containers beside them. It was controlled chaos if that's not a contradiction in terms! And it couldn't go on. A representative of the Inspector of Wireless Telegraphy arrived at the station and, somehow or other, the matter was resolved although I have no recollection of receiving more money. What I do remember is that during that 'work to rule' period of a week or so, I went home absolutely exhausted and, years later, when I taught Trade Unionism to my pupils, I was able to tell them from first hand experience, that 'working to rule' should not be taken lightly! And while all this was going on, the sheep would be grazing in the field outside and 'Cokey', the pure white Persian cat which lived on the Station, might be sprawled across your log!

Portisheadradio received traffic for transmission to ships anywhere in the world. The telegrams came in over the landline teleprinters from all parts of the UK and one of our duties was to put the gummed strips on to telegram forms. You tore off the gummed strip of telegram from the continuous long strip, moistened it on a wet roller and put it on to the form in proper order: first the particulars in the preamble - time, date and office of origin - then the name of the addressee together with the name of the ship - and, finally, the text and the signature. The tearing was done neatly by means of a small, polished metal device with a raised ringed cavity into which you placed your left forefinger if you were right-handed. It had a cutting edge which you pressed down at the relevant part of the gummed strip and severed it with your other hand. The gummed telegrams were then placed into another conveyor-belt channel which took them to the Control Area for sorting out: ships in Areas 1A, 1B and 1C, ships in other Areas, ships classified as passenger ships and foreign vessels. The latter could not, of course, participate in the Area System and had to receive their telegrams direct from Portishead, no matter where they were in the world. The telegrams to other areas were sent on by teleprinter to Whitehall for transmission over the direct naval radio links to any of the other Area Transmitting and Receiving Stations such as Capetown or Sydney, Australia from where they would be broadcast to the ships concerned. There were also the telegrams to ships round the British coasts which could be reached by the coast stations on medium wave. These telegrams were redirected to the relevant coast stations by teleprinter.

The broadcast position was located in the Control Area and the operator on that job was given sufficient time to prepare the broadcast before it went out. First, he had to arrange all the telegrams in alphabetical order according to the ships' call signs. He then made a list of these call signs in the same order and this 'traffic list' preceded the broadcast to let the ship's Radio Officer know if Portisheadradio was about to broadcast a telegram for his ship. The operator could choose to transmit the whole broadcast by hand-key or punch it up on tape and then merely supervise the passage of the tape through the automatic Morse machine. One way was as difficult as the other, but I think most of us usually chose to punch it out on tape as, this way, you got the hard work out of the way earlier in the proceedings. These transmissions were made at 0800-1000, 1200-1400, 1600-1800 and 2000-2200 GMT while at 0000 and 0400 GMT only traffic lists were sent. A telegram was broadcast up to a maximum of six times or until an acknowledgment was received from the ship. If a ship's R/O missed part or all of a telegram, he was at liberty to contact Portishead direct and an operator at an H/F point would send it to him. This facility wasn't known to many of us at sea and we would wait anxiously for the next transmission when, we hoped, conditions would be more favourable. I remember a particular time off the East Coast of Africa in 1946 when my No.2 and I struggled to read the same telegram during several broadcasts. Reception was almost impossible and even when we did have the message complete, we had to call CQ (all stations) on 500 kcs/s to request a ship with H/F to acknowledge it! At that time, all too many ships didn't enjoy the luxury of H/F and when the Area System was scrapped in 1972, a great many shipowners were forced to install H/F transmitters.

Broadcasts were sent at 20 wpm which I consider was exactly right as, after all, that was the speed necessary to qualify for the 2nd Class PMG. One day, however, Eric Macpherson, a close friend of mine, took it upon himself to transmit the broadcast at 25 wpm. He began with a statement informing the R/Os that the broadcast would be sent at 25 wpm and asked for comments! The first I heard of this was when, Archie Madely, one of the older overseers had a brief word with me as he headed for the door and his lunch. "He's just sent the bloody broadcast at 25 wpm! I'm getting the hell out of here," blurted the agitated man. That exercise was never repeated although, strangely enough, I don't think Eric was reprimanded for such a flagrant breach of civil service discipline. One or two complimentary comments did come in, but, of course, there are always some people who have to show off!

The typing of SLTs was a job which expanded or contracted according to the season of the year as they, almost exclusively, contained greetings messages. Like the filing of TRs, this was a job from which a man could be taken if there was pressure on other parts of the system and there were seldom more than two men on this duty. SLTs came into the station in the same way as other telegrams, but, because they were sent on to their destinations from Portishead by post, they qualified for a much cheaper rate. In the 1960s, they cost 10/- for twenty words when full-rate telegrams were 1/8d per word. The SLT was typed on a special attractive form which bore the heading SHIP LETTER TELEGRAM in a light green border with appropriate lightning/wireless flashes. On the left of the form was a drawing of radio masts and the words POST OFFICE TELEGRAPHS VIA PORTISHEAD RADIO. On the right there was a drawing of a passenger liner. The typed SLTs were folded to fit into windowed elongated envelopes and placed into batches for posting according to the desired delivery dates contained in their preambles.

Christmas, of course, was a favourite time for SLTs and I remember particularly the batches which came in from the ships of Salveson's whaling fleet, for posting at Christmas, when they set sail for South Georgia in October. This is another facet of seagoing life which has disappeared, but one which is not to be regretted although the whaling gave much needed employment to many men from Orkney, Shetland and Anglesey.

Christmas Day duties at Portishead, like everything else, were carefully and fairly thought out. Regular duties were suspended. Nobody had the day off, but everybody had part of the day off. A draw was made and you worked during the morning, afternoon or evening. On the first of the two Christmases I was there, I did the morning duty and felt extremely pleased about that. The large Control Area had a wall covered with beautiful Christmas Cards from all over the place.

I neglected to mention that the Control Area had an impressive 36 × 16 feet steel map of the world high up on one of its walls to which magnetic pieces could be attached to indicate the position of ships. It reminded me of the Forces operational maps I'd seen on films, but the only occasion I seem to remember it being used was to plot ships along the route on an occasion when Princess Margaret flew to the West Indies. Incidentally, if a trans-Atlantic aircraft didn't report to its specified airport at a specified time, Portishead would notify ships on its route. This was a safety precaution which had to be taken only occasionally and was likely to mean nothing more than that the 'plane had failed to communicate for some reason.

Telegrams to ships in Area 1 which kept continuous watch i.e. passenger liners, were transmitted at 1015, 1400 and 1800 and not in the main broadcasts which would have been overburdened. Any ship could call up at any time to ask if there was traffic on hand and I think the continuous watch ships were more prone to take advantage of this facility of which, perhaps, most R/Os were ignorant. There was also a long wave frequency available at, I believe, 2 o'clock in the morning. I seem to remember having to ask Criggion for the use of the transmitter and then sending a CQ (all stations) with QRU? (Have you anything for me?) By the fifties, I think this was an anachronism although I believe vessels up the Amazon, perhaps Royal Mail, used to use it.

Ships could request free medical advice from any Post Office Coast Station. The message would be preceded by the Urgency Signal XXX so that the search-point operator gave that ship priority. When the message was received, the ship would be told to standby and the message rushed to the Control Area where someone would immediately 'phone the hospital at Weston-Super-Mare for advice. The advice was then written down, rushed back to the H/F point and transmitted to the waiting ship. Within minutes, a worried Master, far out at sea, could have medical advice on how to treat a sick or injured seaman.

When important people were travelling on ocean liners, we sometimes received reports from the representatives of the Press accompanying them. These press reports, taken in Morse at the H/F points and, usually, but not always, in English, were long and verbose compared to the normal traffic as they were charged at only 1d a word. When Grace Kelly was travelling by sea to marry Prince Rainier in Monaco, screeds came into Portishead regarding every trivial detail which occurred on that ship. The ship called in at a small Spanish port and the mayor came on board to welcome the future Princess Grace. He was kept waiting and was told she would be along shortly. On her way to meet him, she decided to go back to change her dress and, in the long run, she didn't go to meet the man at all although he waited an hour or two. I doubt if that bit of news about the gracious lady ever saw the light of day!

One day, I took a telegram from a Union Castle liner off the coast of South Africa placing a large bet on a horse running at an English race meeting. I particularly noticed this because, when I was at Wick, a bet of £20 from a trawler had caught the attention of everyone at the Station as this was the equivalent of two weeks' wages. That bet had won and we had all regretted not having acted upon the information! A second chance was not to be ignored and Helen sought out a bookmaker in Burnham and placed a bet of ten shillings on the named horse. That horse, needless to say, did not win!

While night duty at Wick was from 11 pm till 9 am, it was from 11 pm till 8 am at Portishead. As the other fellows at Portishead had not worked at Wick, they were unable to appreciate the 8 am finish as I did! At

Portishead too, an overseer might tell you to have break of 20 minutes while, at Wick, this was just impossible. Portishead had a grotty rest room upstairs with tea-making facilities, as tea-breaks (I mean the time made available for your evening meal) were only half an hour and insufficient time to go home. When I visited the Station in later years, they had a large and beautiful place with a modern bar.

A special feature of night duty at Portishead was 'the Draw'. This meant that if, about 3 o'clock in the morning, things went quiet, everyone's name was put into a hat and the person whose name was drawn could go home. I won the draw only once and was on my BSA Bantam and speeding up Worston Lane towards Burnham in no time. Then I realized that I didn't have a door key. The house was a semi-detached villa in Oxford Street, and Helen and I lodged with a family which consisted of the landlady and her daughter and son-in-law. Not wishing to disturb anybody, I raised a side window and began climbing into the room. Entrance, however, was not easy as a large tank of tropical fish stood close to the window and it was slowly and with difficulty that I negotiated this obstacle. I went immediately upstairs and slipped quietly into bed. On rising later that morning, I learned that everybody in the house had been lying in bed listening to my entrance and desperately hoping not to hear the crash of the fish tank!

I don't suppose many R/Os knew that Burnham-on-Sea Radio (GRL) was merely a small position in the landline room of Portisheadradio. I have two memories of operating GRL. One when trying to work a ship in the Bristol Channel area when the R/O's Morse was so slow and bad that I couldn't understand how such an operator had qualified for a 'ticket'. When, after an unsuccessful struggle, I showed my frustration, he sent 'please bare with me' and, of course, I did. The vessel was a survey ship bound for Antarctica and I was told later that, as they had found it impossible to get an R/O to sail in her, she had been accorded 'special dispensation' to allow her to sail without a qualified person. The unqualified man who took the job must have had a hard time and no doubt incurred the wrath of a few coast station operators during his tour of duty.

My other memory of GRL was, on 11 March 1956, taking the final message from the *Deucalion* when she entered Briton Ferry to be broken up. It was strange that, of all those at Portishead, I was the one to take that message.

There were over 90 operators at Portishead when I worked there, but by

1978 there were 220, including two or three women. The increase in staff must have improved the chances of a Pool's win as a 'syndicate' was run very efficiently by an enterprising member of staff who entered a tremendous number of permutations according to the weekly investment. A share cost 1/6d and you could buy as many as you liked. Sometimes the weekly win would be substantial, but there was no payout until the end of the football season and when the winnings were divided out, you might be lucky to break even! It showed me that the chances of a single person winning the Pools are infinitesimal! When paying out, the entrepreneur came round with his tray of small brown envelopes and the recipient signed for his 'winnings'!

The staff at Portisheadradio were as fine a bunch of men as you could hope to meet. As in every large organisation, there were some you didn't care for, but there were far more of the other kind and all of them brought together a fund of stories about the sea that could fill many books. Almost everyone had been in the war and the adventures of that period were almost always recounted in a humorous way. And they knew the world like the backs of their hands. I remember an operator holding a telegram with a Sydney, Australia address which had been garbled. "Anybody know Sydney?" he asked. "Yes, I do," says a bloke. "What's this address meant to be?" asked the holder of the telegram and spelt out the garbled part of the address. "Oh, that's meant to be so and so," said the authority and the matter was cleared up in seconds when referral to the originator of the message would have involved a considerable amount of work plus the consequent delay.

The corollary to my *inability* to attend the Civil Service Commission in London when at Wickradio is quite amusing. Because of the number of men at Portisheadradio who had to be interviewed for Establishment, the Commission came to the Station and the one before which I presented myself came in the summer of 1955.

The Commission consisted of three men; one was a senior member of the Department from London HQ, one was an elderly learned sort of man with white hair and the third was a young man in his thirties. The candidates all came in dressed in their best that day and those on duty were merely relieved at their posts when they were called for interview to the room upstairs where the Commissioners sat behind a long table. When my turn came, I was invited to occupy the chair facing the trio and the interview began with man from the Department asking me questions regarding the job. I don't remember the content of his questions, but I remember that the elderly, scholarly and benign gentleman asked how I occupied my spare time. (I could have said that there wasn't a lot of it!). Among other things, I said that my wife and I went around on our motorbike and enjoyed visiting the many interesting places in the area such as Wells and Glastonbury. This obviously interested the man who then asked if I had noticed the square towers of the churches and understood their significance. I said I knew nothing about this, but he was obviously keen to inform me! When the lesson was over, the young Commissioner, who had been eagerly waiting 'in the wings' and no doubt wondering when the 'old buffer' would stop, launched into his line of questioning which was 'current affairs'. "What newspaper do you get? he asked. "I don't get a newspaper," I replied. This took the wind out of his sails and I could see the other two men derived some amusement from this. It was obvious too that all his further questions were based on me answering his first question by naming a newspaper so that he was momentarily stumped. "Well," he said, "if you do read a newspaper, what interests you? Is it sport?" "I'm not interested in sport," I replied. The other two Commissioners were now enjoying this and the questioner was fumbling. "Well," he said, "what part of a 'paper do you read first?" My answer to that was, "I begin at the beginning and read down." It is probable that I was accepted for Establishment by a two to one vote! But the beauty of it all was that I was not trying to be smart.

I resigned from the Service almost exactly a year later. I have the slip of paper from 'Burnham Radio' which states: "Your notice of resignation dated 4th August 1956 is acknowledged and accepted. Your last day of service will be 24th August 1956". I remember well the reaction to my resignation which can only be described as pique. In no time at all after I had placed my resignation in the O/C's internal mailbox, the Depute O/C came to the H/F point where I was working and asked me to sign the appropriate form. His haste was indecent. There were no pleasantries or 'Won't you reconsider?' It wasn't that I had been inefficient or that the Depute disliked me and, normally, he was an affable man. What rankled was that I was rejecting the Civil Service which, to him, was nigh unforgivable. The Certificate of Character from 'Post Office Radio Station, Highbridge, Somerset' (not Burnham Radio.) states: "....was employed in the Post Office as Radio Operator Class I from the 10th October, 1953 to date (4th August, 1956) when he resigned voluntarily ..... his conduct and performance of duty were satisfactory". An Official Secrets Acts Declaration had to be signed on leaving and I was given a copy of this document which is headed "Declaration to be signed by Members of Government Departments on leaving a Branch or Section concerned with secret work".

I may have given the impression that life at Portishead was so good that it is difficult to understand why I gave up the job. The big drawback was the 6-day week shift work when the hours were never the same for two days running. Meals were taken and snatched at irregular times and the one night-duty a week threw the system out of gear. It was a recipe to undermine health and a few men never lived to draw their pensions. This, however, wasn't my reason for leaving. I just got it into my head that I wanted to be a teacher in Scotland.

I seem to have a clear memory regarding work at the Coast Stations and it has occurred to me that I may have retained a better memory of what it was like at that time because I left the Service. I was there for three years, which was long enough to acquire the mantle of the job and my complete break allows me to remember it as it was. Had I remained in the job until it had changed out of all recognition, my memory of that particular time might not be as clear. Overtaken by more modern technology, Portisheadradio closed at 1200z on Sunday, 30 April, 2000. Wick and all the other coast stations closed at 1200z on Friday, 30 June, in the same year.

In the spring of 1961, I got talking to a chap at the University who, like myself, had previously been a Civil Servant. "You'll be transferring into Teaching?" he asked. I had no idea what he meant so that he explained this was what he was doing under a Scheme which allowed time spent in the Civil Service to be transferred into the Teachers' Superannuation Scheme. I went along to St. Andrews House to investigate this, but was told that the Teachers' Superannuation Department was at Sighthill. I was leaving the building when I noticed a 'phone in the foyer and decided to give the Superannuation Department a call. "Yes," said the lady at the other end, "You can still transfer if you apply to your Department within six months of leaving." "Six months!" I exclaimed, "I've been away for nearly five years!" "Have you been training all that time?" she asked. "Yes," I replied. "The training period doesn't count," she said, "Write to your Department and request permission to transfer into Teaching." And so, almost five years after leaving the Post Office, I wrote asking 'permission to transfer' and 'permission' was granted. I naturally felt pleased about this, but there was the additional satisfaction of knowing that my refusal to make the long journey from Wick to London to see the Commission proved irrelevant, as the whole of my service was transferred into the Teachers' Pension Scheme!

Other seafaring books by Ian M. Malcolm

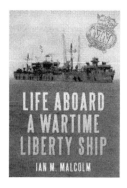

LIFE ON BOARD A WARTIME LIBERTY SHIP
(print and ebook formats, published by Amberley)

Describes the author's wartime experiences as the 3rd Radio Officer of the Liberty Ships *Samite* and *Samforth*.

OUTWARD BOUND (print and ebook formats, published by Moira Brown)

The author's first post-war voyage; on the Liberty Ship *Samnesse*, managed by Blue Funnel for the Ministry of Transport. The voyage begins with calls at Piraeus and Genoa, after which months are spent tramping to various ports in East Africa and the Red Sea. A very happy ship with a predominantly young crew basking in the post-war euphoria.

BACK TO SEA (print and ebook formats, published by Moira Brown)

A voyage to the Far East on the 1911-built *Atreus*, which carries pilgrims to Jeddah on her homeward passage. The author then attends the Lifeboat School in Liverpool and stands by the 1928-built *Eurybates* in Belfast before making his first two voyages on Glen Line's *Glengarry*.

VIA SUEZ (print and ebook formats, published by Moira Brown)

The author makes two more voyages on the *Glengarry* before requesting a voyage to Australia prior to swallowing the anchor. He then coasts the *Glengarry*, *Elpenor/Glenfinlas*, *Helenus*, *Patroclus*, *Medon* and *Clytoneus* after which he is told that his request has been granted. (Photographs/illustrations.)

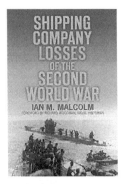

SHIPPING COMPANY LOSSES OF THE SECOND WORLD WAR (print and ebook formats, published by the History Press)

Describes the losses suffered by 53 companies in detail; giving masters' names, where bound, convoy numbers, positions when sunk, casualties and enemy involved.

LETTERS FROM A RADIO OFFICER (print and ebook formats, published by Moira Brown)

Letters sent to the author from a former shipmate who, from 1951 till 1963, served with Brocklebank, Marconi, Redifon (ashore and afloat), the Crown Agents, Clan Line, the Royal Fleet Auxiliary (RFA), Ferranti (in Edinburgh), and Marconi again before settling for a shore job in London.

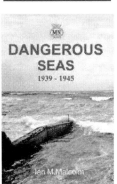

DANGEROUS SEAS (print and ebook formats, published by Moira Brown)

Four book collection – *Dangerous Voyaging, Dangerous Voyaging 2, Fortunes of War* and *Mined Coasts.*

The reader will be left in no doubt of the sacrifices made by the men, and also a few women, of the wartime Merchant Navy.

Printed in Great Britain
by Amazon